Endorsements for *Chopper Warriors*

The Vietnam War – one of the longest, most complex, and controversial in American history – left many citizens uncertain what to think about its origin, length, and its long-range consequences. But an impressive number of American soldiers who actually fought in the conflict are determined to make sure that the public will have abundant documentation of the will courage, ingenuity, and brotherly valor daily invested in each other's lives and their country's honor.

One of those candid, tell-it-like-it-was authors is Bill Peterson – born and raised in the Upper Peninsula of Michigan. In this second book, *Chopper Warriors,* he has joined mind and memory with fellow veterans to tell one of the most remarkably thorough accounts of the war in the long years that haunted the nation.

—*Ed Lambeth, Professor Emeritus*
University of Missouri School of Journalism

I met Bill through a mutual friend. Talking with Bill about his time in Viet Nam and the time I spent there, we found that we had many things in common. Reading his first book *Missions of Fire and Mercy* brought back many memories. Some of them I had pushed to the far back of my mind and forgotten. For those who have never been in any branch of the military or been in a war zone, Bill's first book *Missions Of Fire and Mercy* and his new book *Chopper Warriors* are must reads. They give an insight into the daily life of what it is like to be in an Army Aviation unit in combat. Once you start reading, you will not want to put them down until you reach the end. The Viet Nam veterans are finally being shown some of the respect that they should have been given years ago. I pray that no other American Service Personnel are treated in that manner ever again. I am looking forward to reading the entire *Chopper Warriors* book.

—*James C. DuBose, Jr. CW-4 Army Retired*

Authentic writing of real life experience of wartime. Compelling with an insight given only from someone who lived it.

—Jimmy Westmoreland, Vietnam 1967-1969

Bill Peterson's book, *Missions of Fire and Mercy,* is filled with thrilling and technically accurate day-to-day descriptions of his tour and experiences as a crew chief in Vietnam. He is a gifted storyteller who writes no "fluff copy". His attention to detail is outstanding, and in the end he is able to make a great page turning story out of the not so great "Vietnam Conflict". His award winning *Missions of Mercy and Fire* resonates with history and invokes both good and bad memories of the 60's and 70's. I cannot wait for the newest installment *Chopper Warriors*. It is guaranteed to be a historically accurate look at our involvement in Viet Nam through Bill's eyes and experiences.

—Jim Tertin, Director of Manufacturing
Magnum Research

Author Bill Peterson is a great storyteller! His writing style is down to earth and easy to read. The author's last award-winning book, *Missions of Fire and Mercy,* is compelling, riveting, and an educational tome – a story of remarkable courage. I look forward to reading more from this author."

—John Podlaski, Author
Cherries - A Vietnam War Novel

As Bill's "big sister", I could not be more proud of your accomplishments! Bill, you are my personal hero. Until you wrote your harrowing stories of Viet Nam in *Missions of Fire and Mercy,* I had never really heard your heart concerning that war. Cindi is amazing for loving you through your nightmares for so many years. Now that you are writing your memories, there is fresh relief and a new kind of healing – not just for you, Bill, but for all your readers who shared that horrific war.

That God has gifted you with so many wonderful talents, in addition to writing, is an inspiration to all who know you. You have made more with what God has given than anyone else I know. Your life of faith consistently reflects the glory of God and His amazing creation. I know you will one day hear, "Well done, good and faithful servant!"

—Fran Lambeth

I just had an opportunity to review excerpts from Bill Peterson's new book, *Chopper Warriors*. For those of us who read Bill's first book, *Missions of Fire and Mercy,* this new book continues to share many new and gripping stories based on his experiences as a helicopter gunner during the Vietnam War. Bill writes in a straightforward, down to earth manner about life in a war zone. His work is honest, personal, and real. When I read his stories it becomes clearer to me why so many of our veterans come home with PTSD and why it is so important for our nation to only send our young people into war when there is a very compelling reason. I highly recommend Mr. Peterson's new book, *Chopper Warriors*, to readers who wish to better understand life on a helicopter gun ship and the personal sacrifices associated with combat.

—Gerald Goffin

Bill Peterson has done it again. His first book, *Missions of Fire and Mercy,* is a classic about the helicopter war during the Vietnam conflict. One of the best in my library. Now his second book is even better. I know it is going to bless you as it has me. We were both soldiers once...and young.

—Chief Warrant Officer & former helicopter pilot
Vietnam, 1969-1970. 25th Infantry Division
Dr. Joseph Wasmond, Living Legacy International

I first met Bill in 1979 when I relocated to his tiny hometown of Carney, Michigan. Our wives had gotten to know each other at the small rural church that our young families attended, and through the church we became close friends. I was immediately impressed with Bill's humor and his quiet, humble, forthright personality. At the time I met Bill he had been building log homes and was running a small trucking business with his brother.

Although I had been in the military during the mid 60's and early 70's, for some reason the subject of military service never came up for several years. It wasn't until my wife mentioned that Bill's wife, Cindi, had spoken of the military service medals Bill earned while serving in Viet Nam that I became aware of the horrific battle experiences he had been through. Bill's low-key personality had never exhibited any hint of the firefights he had been in.

When I broached the topic with Bill he quietly replied that thousands of others had also been through it, and many with less fortunate outcomes.

Bill's written accounts of his combat experiences convey to the reader the realization that our country has thousands of unsung military heroes walking among us who deserve our deepest gratitude and respect.

Thank you, Bill, and all of our military veterans.

—*Rich Nichols, Wisconsin*

Mr. Peterson has done it again...two books in a row that are "must reads"! In his first book, *Missions of Fire and Mercy: Until Death Do Us Part*, he chronicles his year in Viet Nam, 1967-68, as a Crew Chief and Door Gunner in an UH1H "Huey" helicopter. Through the seemingly innocent device of his letters home (saved by his parents and girlfriend) Mr. Peterson draws you into the intense battle horrors that transformed him from an innocent, naïve midwestern boy into a battle hardened combat hero!

His current book, *Chopper Warriors*, demonstrates both his maturation as an author and his personal growth in dealing with his lifelong struggle with the aftermath of that year of combat...PTSD. If anything, Mr. Peterson's ability to describe vividly the horrors and fears of intense combat has become even more graphic. *Chopper Warriors* is an anthology of combat experiences lived both by himself and other veterans whom he interviewed. Each episode leaps off the page because of Mr. Peterson's vivid narrative skill that immerses you, the reader, in that epic struggle between fear and personal courage that every combat veteran must face. This ultimate moral dilemma and personal struggle is as relevant today and to our current veterans of Iraq and Afghanistan and their families as it was to veterans and their loved ones experiencing the social upheaval of the Viet Nam era. And, no one describes that struggle and the horror of intense combat as well as Mr. Peterson. *Chopper Warriors* must be read by all who wish to truly experience empathy for the young men we send off to foreign lands and into combat!

—Gordon L. Carr, Ph.D.
Clinical Psychologist (ret.)

OTHER AWARD WINNING BOOKS BY AUTHOR

Missions Of Fire And Mercy – Until Death Do Us Part

WRITING HONORS

Missions Of Fire And Mercy, a memoir, is a Silver Medal Winner from The Military Writers Society of America (MWSA).

AVAILABLE ON

www.missionsoffireandmercy.com
www.chopperwarriors.com

Chopper Warriors

Kicking the Hornet's Nest

WILLIAM E. PETERSON

Dedication

Far too many families have gone through the pain of losing one or more of their sons, daughters, fathers, husbands or grandchildren in wars that span the globe.

The stories you are about to read are about many of those heroes who fought not only for their lives, but also for the lives of others, and for the freedoms we enjoy today in America.

I salute each of you for your sacrifice to our nation.

Acknowledgements

The men whose names appear under each chapter heading are my heroes. While listening to each of their stories, I was mesmerized by the honesty, sincerity, and even humor. Though I really didn't want to take these soldiers back to the horrors they experienced some 45+ years ago, it was necessary to be able to correctly portray their combat experiences in Viet Nam. Like me, their short-term memory is considerably less than perfect. On the other hand, combat is seared into the brain to the extent it will never be forgotten. We were young and very green at first. Soon we lived the lives of soldiers, of Chopper Warriors, and necessarily became combat savvy at a huge and enduring price in order to stay alive.

Combat soldiers carry a lot of unseen baggage. That baggage is not like all the pastel colors you see on airport suitcases. It is, instead, very gray and often black, steeped in thick sticky red. It is not seen by the average citizen, but is viewed by the combat soldier almost every day that he/she is alive.

I am grateful for the willingness of these men to let me bore into their past. It is my honor to know each of them.

I am grateful to all crewmembers with whom I served, many of who gave all to save others. You are all truly my brothers in blood.

To all my brothers and sisters who served in Viet Nam, your service was less than appreciated by your national family – you volunteered, you served when called, you gave your best and I salute you.

I want to thank my family for allowing me the time to write when I certainly had a long list of projects that needed to be done. Thanks to my son, Jeremy who was often able to steer me in the right direction when I was overwhelmed with computer issues. My daughter, Jennifer was very helpful in helping me with editing. Cindi, my wife of 45 years, has stood beside me in all my endeavors. She is a very patient, understanding and loving wife. I am very thankful that God gave me such a precious gift. I am very proud to have been married for 45 years.

My editor, Remy Benoit, ('Miz Remy') as she is affectionately called, is very capable in her trade. Being an author, historian, teacher, publisher, and editor, she has a lot of experience in dealing with editing details. Remy has a big heart for Veterans.

Editor's Note

When we of the Viet Nam generation were children, helicopters were awe-inspiring.

We squealed, jumped about, pointed upward yelling, "Look, look"!

Over the decades, helicopters and their crews became so much more to so many. They became, as Bill Peterson so aptly put it – *Missions of fire and mercy.*

Those of us at home during the Viet Nam Era truly were not aware of the vast extent of what the choppers and their pilots meant to those in combat. One medic who served in the AO of Cu Chi estimated that that number of names listed on the Vietnam Memorial would be 10X higher than the 58,195 names now listed on it – **TEN TIMES higher.**

God Bless the Chopper Warriors and all they gave to bring life saving ammo, food, medical supplies, medevacs, and hope. Think of it, there you are in the monsoon rains, in temps at 130 with matching humidity, surrounded by VC or NVA troops – hungry, wounded, out of ammo and the sweet sound of those rotors reminds you that you are not facing the living hell of war alone. Your buddy, gut ripped, legs missing has only moments, and that smoke is popped, that flight crew risks all to get him medevaced and

healed enough with that million dollar wound to go home. It might not be the homecoming he dreamed of, his sweetheart wrote of, but he would be going home because of a handful of men absolutely dedicated, on flight duty that was VOLUNTARY, followed that popped smoke in the abyss of defoliated jungle and screaming men.

Some of those crews, the Ranch Hand crews, sprayed what they were told would not harm them as it back washed all over them from the rotors. What they sprayed was Agent Orange or some other color; what they lived with, died with, was the effect of that defoliant. Of the c. 3,000,000 who served in Viet Nam, c. 800,000 are still with us.

As the American War in Viet Nam wound down, M.A.S.H. introduced the civilian population to the efficacy of those choppers in bringing soldiers to life saving triage every time that Radar hollered in Korea: *INCOMING.*

Bill Peterson and the other authors who have shared their days and nights of war give you a whole new meaning, a fearful insight to the multiple meanings of *INCOMING.*

It meant bringing grunts to medical help; it also meant grunts under fire. To the chopper crews it meant the literal rotor and prayer, flying into a hot LZ just one bullet away from a fiery crash.

To all the Chopper Warriors, thank you for keeping those KIA numbers as low as possible until we learn a better way than war.

It has been my privilege and pleasure to work with Bill Peterson. What he and his co-authors are telling you is important. Open your eyes, see in part what they have known, and help find a better legacy for our young than war.

It has been said that war is a failure of diplomacy. Interestingly, we have all kinds of 'therapy' for other kinds of communication breakdowns to prevent violence and death. Perhaps we need to think about ways to nurture diplomacy, communication, to spare lives, and avoid destruction. Perhaps we owe that to our young before we send them to serve. Just a thought to consider.

—Remy Benoit

Preface

After having written my first Award Winning book, *Missions Of Fire And Mercy*, I felt something was missing. I have always had a great deal of respect for the Infantry (grunts) who our unit, C/227th Assault Helicopter Battalion, 1st Air Cavalry supported. They were always appreciative of the helicopters and crews. My personal feeling is that they heroically fought the worst part of the Viet Nam war.

Chopper Warriors will introduce many of the survivors of that war. The interesting, and often thrilling stories you are about to read are from men whom I am honored to know. Many of the words written here are theirs from interviews I have done. As a storyteller, I have tried to recapture the events as they happened forty-five plus years ago.

The narrative and scenes created here are mostly true, and the dialogue is written for all audiences from teenagers to adults, men and women alike.

Our unit supported these men in every way; inserting them into the fiery hell of battle, and supplying them with ammo, food, water, and mail, often under intense enemy fire. When they were ready to move on to a different LZ, we picked them up and re-inserted them. When they were sick or wounded, we flew them to the closest field hospital. When they were silently lying in the jungle, having breathed their last, they were solemnly picked up and loaded on our choppers. We reverently evacuated them to an area where they could be cared for, prior to their final flight back to their loved ones. I have the utmost respect for the guys we called "grunts".

Though our military technology didn't always work, the helicopter was a very useful tool for putting our troops right where they needed to be – deep within the enemy's lair. More importantly, the choppers saved innumerable lives that in other wars would have been snuffed out. For that I am grateful to have been a part of the First Team in Viet Nam.

In my personal stories that you will read, I have used actual names whenever possible. In other cases, names have been changed in honor of the families.

It is my most sincere hope that these accounts will be read by many who have lost loved ones in this most unpopular war. Many soldiers involved in Viet Nam, the Gulf War, Iraq, Afghanistan, and others have declined to tell their own stories to those they love back home, as they actually happened. The feelings that war veterans have run very deep and are often very traumatic. Many don't want to relive those horrendous nightmares. Severe cases of PTSD, guilt, or not wanting families to know what they went through are prevalent and very real.

In many cases, their stories are relived here as they actually happened. Here, you may finally read about what your son, grandson, husband, father, or friend endured. Though honorable and often heroic, you can be sure the memories are horrible, and something they will never forget.

Throughout this document, you will see the word "grunts." It seems that all wars have their own nomenclature. In Viet Nam, a grunt fought the toughest part of the war, in my mind.

In many cases, that was to lessen the fear of their family and friends. Though noble, I personally feel that to be a shame. I pray that knowing what your loved ones went through may bring healing to a lot of you.

Contents

CHAPTER 1

William E. Peterson

Puff

At 0100 a battalion of North Vietnamese Regulars emerge on their bellies from the surrounding jungle. Low crawling through the grass and brush toward the perimeter manned by Bravo, 1/9th Cav., they're itching for a fight. In all likelihood, they're all probably doped up on either marijuana, or a multitude of hard drugs. This helps them fight without so much fear. This also makes them more difficult for the Americans to fight. The American encampment is probed with sporadic small arms fire at 0130 hours. The entire company within the perimeter is on full alert, expecting a ground attack. At 0150, incoming mortars lead the fierce NVA charge. Bugles sound just prior to the enemy launching their full-scale assault. Knowing that the NVA often use bugles, it still peaks the hairs on the back of your neck that are already raised. Goose bumps join the incredible adrenaline flow when you know a battle with the enemy is imminent. Quickly realizing that the attacking soldiers far outnumber the dug-in grunts, at the sound of the first note blown on the bugle, Company Commander, Captain Thurmond "Bullnose Two", commands his troops to, "Fix bayonets!" He's calling for immediate air support. Fortunately the Air Force has just finished sweeping up another operation nearby, when they're alerted that their services are desperately needed once again.

The Gooks are feeling frisky tonight and are attacking several firebases in the immediate area. Bravo Company is an incredible fighting force, using its full firepower potential in an attempt to hold off the tenacious NVA soldiers. The concertina wire is breached on the west side. The enemy is in a full court press in their attempt to wipe out the company of grunts who have been vigorously patrolling the area. The American infantrymen have been a sharp thorn in Charlie's butt by ambushing and killing twenty-three of their men during the past several days.

A disturbed bee's nest of blazing yellow tracers spits out of the offside of the aircraft overhead. It's the only (and most welcome) sound heard, as "Puff the Magic Dragon" breathes death onto the soldiers of the north. The blacked out C47 gunship, blasts the perimeter of the LZ with its lethal mini-guns.

A normal pass with one mini-gun is capable of putting one round in every square foot of a football field. Puff uses three of these. Even though every fifth round of M60 ammo is a tracer, the Gatling guns spout a trail of lead that appears as a solid stream of screaming and haunting yellowish-orange death bent on destroying everything in their path. Covering every inch of ground where the weapons are directed outside of the perimeter, few of the enemy soldiers escape annihilation. Our tax dollars are at work...for a most worthy cause. Gunpowder has never smelled so sweet!

Following a twelve to fifteen minute nighttime attack, the crew of the C47 is called out for another mission. Good timing, since it appears that the ground attack has been called off with many enemy soldiers lying on the ground. The majority of the enemy is either wiped out, or has escaped into the jungle. One thing is for sure, those left standing are more scared than they've ever been after escaping death by the Dragon.

"Bullnose Two, Scattergun Four has been called for another mission. I think we've spoiled the fun down there for now. Give us a ring if ya'll need us again."

"Scattergun Four, you've saved our necks again and we can't thank you enough."

"No problem, Bullnose. More than happy to oblige. Stay safe now, 'ya hear?"

By 0310 the badly shot up LZ is cloaked in a blanket of pungent smelling cordite smoke. The nerve-shattered American troops prowl about in search of any of the enemy that might still be inside the perimeter. The churned up earth is streaked, spattered and smeared with the precious blood of soldiers from both sides. Parts of bodies are even found.

It's an extremely active night in the area north and west of Camp Evans. The enemy has suffered terrific losses, while the Americans who fought so bravely take stock, and find they've suffered three dead comrades with seven others wounded. A call for an immediate medevac is received by C/227 Assault Helicopter Co, lst Cav at Camp Evans. The Charlie Company Flight Operations Specialist Larry Lizotte, calls Bravo Company Flight Ops to alert them to fly gunship cover for the Slicks.

Rousted out of our bunks, our flight crews jump into our flying clothes and run to the Flight Ops tent to get a quick mission brief. The brief includes the current situation at the LZ; coordinates, radio freqs, call signs and weather. After a rough jeep ride up the dust-covered trail to the revetments protecting the assigned aircraft, the crews jump out. It's an extremely hot and muggy night. We all feel and look like we've just come out of a sauna. The dust has settled on all of us, so basically, we're covered with mud before we even begin the mission. Untying the main rotor blades, I do a quick walk around inspection with my flashlight.

Gunner Sammy Davidson ("Squirrel") mounts the two machine guns and loads the ammo trays on both sides of the bird with 2500 rounds of belted 7.62mm ammo. For good measure, he puts another thousand rounds under each gunner's seat. The extremely skinny "Squirrel" came to us from Newark, New Jersey. Admitting to being the member of a former gang, he attempts to be a pretty tough guy. That doesn't work with the rest of our crew. We all work as a team. Squirrel will either become an active team member or we'll send him back to the jungle where he came from. We can easily see right through his smoke screen. Who knows, this flight may straighten him out. He's a former grunt who has tired of slogging through the mud and being shot at, so he did a six month extension of his tour, enabling him to have orders cut to be a chopper door gunner. This is his first mission. He is assuming that receiving machine gun fire won't be so bad in a chopper. We'll see how he does under fire while airborne. It's always interesting to see the reaction of a new gunner when they start seeing bullets come through the floor between their feet, and of course, in some cases they're wounded...or worse.

While the second crew boards their ship next to my old reliable "092", we're ready to go and co-pilot, six-foot Warrant Officer George Eastwood fires up our bird. The Aircraft Commander, Captain Joe Stringer, is talking to flight ops for last minute instructions. He sports a lengthy jet-black handlebar mustache and is called "Sasquatch" by most of the enlisted men and the other warrant officers. His large frame waddles somewhat from side to side when he walks, and has enough hair covering it to have gorillas as close ancestors. Officially, he is "Ghostrider One Two."

Stringer calls his wingman Ghostrider One Five and the Cobra flight of two.

"Ghostrider One Five, you up?

"Ghostrider One Five ready to go."

"Sharpshooter Flight, Ghostrider One Two, you up?"

"Ghostrider One Two, Sharpshooter Seven and Nine up, and ready."

"Evans Tower, Ghostrider One Two, flight of four request departure to the north from Charlie and Bravo company pads."

"Ghostrider One Two, cleared to the north as requested. Wind is out of the southwest at three."

"Roger, cleared to the north. Thank you."

"Have a safe flight Ghostrider One Two."

With four aircraft mixing it up on this ebony colored night, all exterior nav lights are left on in an attempt to avoid any mid-air collisions.

The Charlie Company Slicks take the lead, departing to the north with the Cobras joining them in trail. A ten-minute flight puts the four aircraft within four miles of the LZ, and we can see faint fires in the distance where the battle is taking place. All aircraft are ordered to turn out all exterior nav lights to avoid detection by the enemy, and to follow flight separation rules. Just before this is done, the pilots automatically increase their distance from the aircraft ahead for an extra margin of safety. We must also adhere to air speeds now that were discussed at the mission briefing. If an aircraft is too fast or too slow, the result could quickly become a fiery crash. Our crews must be super diligent to avoid a mid-air collision.

Climbing through 2500 feet, Captain Stringer calls to the Ground Commander at the besieged LZ.

"Bullnose Two, Ghostrider One Two is four miles south. Flight of four en-route your location. SITREP please."

"Roger Ghostrider One Two. LZ cold at this time. No wind, but there is some residual smoke hanging over our location."

"We have seven WIAs and three KIAs."

"Roger. Have a ground guide in the landing area with a strobe light. We'll be approaching straight in from the south, one ship at a time. Blacked out. We can see the tracers going in and out. LZ in sight."

Radio transmissions are always abbreviated. Particularly when a flight is on a major mission and the enemy is banging away in an attempt to bag a chopper. It seems like half of the men are trying to talk on the radio, with enemy gun position reports, reporting that they're receiving fire and from where, aircraft is hit badly, crew member is wounded, and maintenance issues that require returning to base or having to land nearby in the beehive. In the mix of course are frightening Mayday calls. These always take precedence. These crews need attention, and they need it right now. Should they go down we will make every attempt to get them out immediately. If the enemy fire is too fierce, a plan is quickly formulated and additional troops or aircraft are put on the scene.

No man left behind is of utmost importance to all of us. We know that if our aircraft has to make an emergency landing or crashes, our comrades will be there for us. They will risk their very lives to save us. They know we will do the same for them. There are missions when trying to get even one man out may result in another aircraft shot down. All too often, another brother sacrifices his life to save a comrade in deep trouble.

The eerie glow of burning tents and bunkers in the distance appears through the licorice colored night. This has been the last stand for three more young American men who have suffered grisly deaths.

When a half mile from the battle site, we see the strobe light held by the ground guide. The Slicks break into a trail formation with a two-minute separation. This should be enough to allow Charlie Company to load its precious cargo.

The two Cobras slide just to the rear and on either side of the lead ship. Fingers draw a little tighter on the triggers. We're all just waiting for trouble any second. We're all exhausted from flying thirteen hours the previous day, but we must stay sharp.

The pilots flying the mission use the last known altimeter setting. This measures barometric pressure. The chart has been scanned for the approximate elevation of the planned LZ. With that as a target, the pilots can calculate how high they must be on the approach to avoid a collision with either the ground or trees. The early morning darkness is reason for the birds to make a high approach to the LZ.

Approaching the unknown, our nerves draw as tight as a bowstring. Guns at the ready, we don't plan on suppressing the enemy unless we're fired upon and are able to detect the exact enemy location. We're unsure of the layout of the LZ, and night approaches are always filled with terror. There are too many variables added to the blackness. Working as a crew, we're always searching for trees and rock outcroppings, not to mention enemy fire. The unseen tree lines surrounding the LZ stand as sentinels ready to strike with terror should a helicopter become entangled in its long reaching tentacles, bringing a crew of four young men to a premature grave.

There's a thin layer of smoke in the area from the battle. When the strobe is spotted, the first slick is on short final and lands in a whirl of dust. Five casualties are hastily loaded on board our ship. Even in the dim glow of the cabin lights, I catch a glimpse of the eyes of those shirtless men loading the wounded. Though not wounded yet, the unreal fear in their dilated eyes is unlike anything I've ever seen. I'm mesmerized by the look and terror each of these men is wearing on their blood-smeared, bruised and mud-caked faces. Seeing the nature of the severe injuries, tears stream down my cheeks. This is a natural reaction for me whenever we evacuate the wounded.

Over the past few hours, these brave boys have become battle-hardened men. This has been a fixed bayonet, toe-to-toe fight that will haunt them the rest of their lives.

With a thumbs-up from the ground guide, our chopper departs to the east under automatic weapons fire, with several rounds finding their mark. The pinging and sharp snare drum sounds can be heard throughout the aircraft. Squirrel and I return fire at the muzzle flashes, while Bravo company pilots roll in on the enemy's tracers with their Cobras. We turn on course toward the field hospital at Evans.

Immediately following our departure, Ghostrider One Five lands his bird into a fray of gunfire that has now opened up on the LZ. The remainder of the Grunts are dead. They're loaded quickly and their aircraft makes a quick retreat, while being fired upon and also taking several hits.

"Ghostrider One Five, receiving small arms and automatic weapons fire from the tree line on the edge of the LZ."

"Roger, we'll hose them down for 'ya."

One Cobra is passing over the LZ at the time of the call and the other is trailing our second bird number two. The one following the slick that has just been shot up happily cuts loose with his mini-guns, while the second Cobra does a quick turn to the left and pumps four rockets into the same place. They each make one more pass, attempting to extinguish the danger to the unit on the ground before returning to the flight of two medevac ships. Cobra crews are known to be trigger-happy. Just doing their job, doing it with extreme pride, and maybe just a bit of vengeance.

While enroute to Evans, I use my flashlight to check our unfortunate passengers. Four of the seven men are seriously wounded. One of these young boys is missing his left leg and the majority of his right arm. His eyes are the size of dinner plates, and though he had been administered morphine by the medic on the ground, he's in shock. I wonder if shock might be God's way of reducing the pain, temporarily. Another soldier is left with a gaping wound in his left shoulder. Patient number three has severe shrapnel wounds all across his face and chest. The last severely injured comrade is missing half of his right foot. The other men have shrapnel and bullet wounds. Needless to say, the KIAs on the second aircraft have sadly completed their tours of duty. They have valiantly fought their final battle, and will be counted amongst the thousands of young heroes who lost their dreams, their hopes, and their lives, so that others may enjoy their freedom back in America. I grieve deeply for their families and loved ones.

Whenever death is encountered, even if the comrade is unknown, grieving takes place by all who see him. It's only natural, I guess, regardless of who we are. We feel badly for our Brothers and their loved ones. The problem is that our flights as chopper crews are often short. As soon as we land, we will likely have to concentrate on another mission. All of these flights demand our total attention. One split second of inattentiveness can mean severe injury or death to all of us.

After delivering the dead and wounded to the hospital pad, our mission is complete. We return to our aircraft revetments where our birds will be somewhat protected from flying shrapnel until our next mission.

Camp Evans receives a lot of incoming mortar and rocket fire almost daily. Though we never know when the rounds are coming, the majority whistle in after dark. Our aircraft are often spattered with shrapnel, or destroyed by direct hits when a revetment is of no protection. On an aircraft, especially a chopper, there are many critical parts. Even a nick found on any of these can ground the aircraft. If a replacement part is available, our maintenance crews usually have the bird back up within hours. Oftentimes another part is pirated from one of our other damaged birds. In some cases the part must be flown in from another base. Occasionally, it's unavailable within the country and it must be ordered directly from Bell Helicopter in Dallas, Texas.

When the whoosh, whoosh, whoosh sounds of the rotor blades stop, I see "Squirrel" coming my way with a look of determination.

"Pete, I've had enough experience as a gunner on one mission to have made up my mind to go back and hump the boonies. I was terrified when I heard those rounds hit the chopper. I found out there's no place to hide in a chopper. At least I can hide behind a tree, rock, or dike when I'm in the field. I'm gonna talk to the First Sergeant right after breakfast about getting some new orders cut to go back to my old unit."

"OK, man. No sweat. If you have any buddies that would like to give it a try, have them get in contact with us. We're always looking for gunners. I guess by now, you can understand why."

I crawl all over my ship looking for more bullet holes that may need to be patched, oil, fuel, or hydraulic leaks that need attention, main or tail rotor strikes, or shrapnel nicks in any of the flight controls. Missing any one of these items can mean a catastrophic flight. We always try to find our problems on the ground. Any time we've been badly shot up, the gunner and pilots lend additional pairs of eyeballs to help spot anything the crew chief may have missed. Upon inspection, I find five AK47 holes in the tail boom and one through the left door of the ship. None of the rounds have penetrated anything crucial, including the crew, so they can wait until I have time to patch them with sheet metal. They don't need attention tonight. I'm beat!

So many young men suffering and dying is making a definite imprint on my mind and body. Flight status is voluntary and I am not required to fly. However, I feel a strong connection to the men we serve in the field everyday. We have to take them on combat assaults, but then we fly ammo, food, water, and mail out to them as needed. And then come the all too numerous days and nights when we have to medevac the wounded, screaming, and dying.

Sometimes, we're just on a ride over gorgeous country at tree top level. Unfortunately, most days are far from pleasant. They require nerves of steel, perseverance, guts and a lot of prayer. We're often under great pressure to get the supplies out to our men who are pinned down and running low on ammo, have heavy casualties, and need immediate evacuation. Often we can hear soldiers desperately crying out on the radio for help. Whenever I hear those voices my heart breaks. We get there as quickly as we can, but sometimes that isn't fast enough.

If we arrive right after or during a gunfight, we often see a ghostly site of blood and bodies scattered throughout the LZ. There are times when we chopper crew's work around the clock. We're physically, mentally, and emotionally drained. Will this madness ever stop?

The Grunts need us, and to a fault, we're dedicated to helping our fellow comrades! We do everything within our means to get in and rescue anyone who calls for emergency aid. Most of the time, we receive enemy fire. A wounded warrior is like a decoy for rescue birds. Sometimes our crewmembers are wounded, or even killed in that attempt. All too often our choppers, or those supporting us are shot down. But...we do everything we can to leave no man behind.

Tomorrow's another day. It may prove to be more memorable than today.

CHAPTER 2

Larry Troxel

Saddle Up

During my second tour, while our company awaits extraction, we hear a gaggle of fourteen choppers coming over the ridge. We're already formed up in fourteen groups of seven men ready to load up for a search and destroy mission.

After a short eight-minute flight we're within a half click of the Cambodian border. When I realize we're going on a mission so close to the enemy's known stronghold in Cambodia, I feel myself getting much more uneasy than on most missions. We Americans have been chasing the enemy all over this country, where we have wounded and killed thousands. Now we're going into one of their likely hornet's nests. My gut tells me we may be getting into a battle where we may not be victorious. I've never felt like this. Our unit is a fantastic team and we have won every battle we've fought. When I envision the possibilities, my mind conjures up many of us being maimed for life and others on their very last mission. I'm spooked beyond comprehension.

On approach to a rice paddy large enough to enable all of our birds to land at the same time, we see that the paddy is on the outskirts of a small village. Fortunately, we meet no incoming enemy fire; intelligence suspects this area to contain NVA, although estimated numbers are unknown to us. Often they'll wait to spring the attack when we have no nearby helicopter support.

As always, upon exiting the choppers, our company scrambles for position in the nearby tree line to provide covering fire for the departing helicopters. The enemy must be taking a siesta. There is still no enemy fire. It's way too quiet. This is spooky. Where are they?

After we're settled in on full alert, the stillness is eerie. It just doesn't seem quite right. Even though we see villagers moving about in this remote jungle hamlet, our study with field glasses doesn't pose any immediate threats. There are mostly small grass huts with a couple of larger ones on the northeast corner. Children, women, old men, chickens, pigs, and a few water buffalo skirt this quaint picture post card. We can't see any older boys or able-bodied men. This is business as usual; teenage boys and healthy men are generally "recruited" (forcibly) by the local NVA to join them in their fight against America and its Allies.

After spreading out, we begin searching through the village. We're looking expectantly and nervously into every hut for contraband items, for caches of weapons under the dirt floors of the hootches, and searching for possible hiding places such as spider holes and tunnel entrances–nerve wracking. The local inhabitants seem nervous...like they're trying to hide something.

We're all on edge.

When reaching the far corners of the village, we discover why they're nervous. We find a huge NVA base camp.

While working slowly, we're moving through the base camp when we still hear that dreaded silence. Spotting a very large fortified, bunker we pause to quietly discuss a plan to destroy it and anyone who may be inside.

Two of my comrades and I low crawl to within thirty-five yards, when we hear laughing coming from the well-fortified bunker in front of us.

Weird.

Before we light it up with the M60, we scan the jungle to see if we're being watched by anyone. Not twenty feet to the left of the bunker lay a Gook in a hammock. He hasn't spotted or heard us yet.

My M16 finds its mark. The enemy soldiers in the bunker are still laughing like they're partying. It appears they haven't heard the report of my rifle. SP4 Ronnie Johnson and I sneak to within twelve to fifteen feet of the bunker entrance while SP4 Rodriquez stays back to cover us, should we be discovered.

Both Ronnie and I lob grenades through the door. Within a couple seconds, they're returned to us! A savvy enemy is in there and spotted the grenades immediately. These frags are about timed out and ready to explode! Diving for cover behind a natural berm, we hit the ground just as both grenades cook off simultaneously, with no one injured, including those in the bunker. However, the party ends at the sound of the American frags, and three NVA troops come running out with their AKs. They're so doped-up; they don't even take a peek first to see where all the commotion is coming from. They begin flappin' their sandals wide open for the jungle when our men draw down and shoot them. We light the place up with M16s and our M60.

End of story.

Almost.

When the smoke clears, Ronnie and I carefully check out the inside of the bunker to see what was so funny. Lying on the floor in the far right corner are over twenty packs of opium. Party's over gang.

After we take only a couple of steps, enemy mortars begin exploding all around us. Several of us dive for the bunker we've just cleared. The rest of the company takes cover wherever they can. Just after the mortars begin to drop, two of our men are severely wounded. Our RTO is calling in our coordinates for immediate air power and a "dust off" chopper.

"Snakespit One, Alpha Two under heavy mortar attack. Request immediate airstrike, over."

"Roger Alpha Two, Flight of two Cobras inbound your position. We have a couple of Skyraiders tagging along if you want them."

"Most definitely Snakespit, we'll take everything we can get!"

"Rog, ETA four minutes."

The screams of pain from our rifleman and mortarman are heard above the din of the battle. Now included in the mortar fire is the sound of AKs with enemy light machine gun fire included. We're laying out fire as fast as we can, while awaiting WR6 to deliver our life saving air power.

We don't have to wait long before we hear the "whoosh, whoosh, whoosh...whoosh" of aerial rocket fire around our position. The ultra-smooth rotation of the four six-barreled mini-guns is bringing a fiery hell to the scrambling NVA!

Two A1E Skyraiders screaming down from the cloudless sky are turning up the heat while dropping two 500# canisters each of napalm onto the fleeing enemy. The A1Es flown by South Vietnamese pilots are prop-driven, relatively slow, and therefore deadly accurate. On a second pass they join in with rocket, canon, and machine gun fire. The smoke from the gunpowder thickens.

We're all cheering since we aren't receiving any more enemy rounds. The NVA are weary of the battle, and are either hunkered down trying to escape almost certain death, or running for their lives through the jungle.

Though "cheering" may sound barbarian to many who have never experienced heavy combat, please try to understand. Our company has just gone through another horrible battle and has two more buddies who are WIA. With all the losses our company has experienced, both wounded and dead, those of us who have survived to this point, feel like we may be next. One step away from your own grave is a horrible feeling. We want revenge.

"Saddle up, we're gettin' outa' here. We're over the Red Line" (over the Cambodian border), says LT.

Two Cobras are laying down a smoke screen for the slicks that are following, hoping to escape enemy fire. The enemy who have held their ground are experiencing the wrath of American and Allied firepower at its best.

Can victory get any better than this?

CHAPTER 3

William Peterson

Confidential

One of the required daily tasks that's required of every unit in a war zone is to have the Duty Officer or Company Clerk stand by the radio and record the activities of the unit for every twenty-four hour period. This record is called the "Daily Staff Journal or Duty Officer's Log". These reports during my tour are now declassified.

These daily logs are handwritten, and as you might imagine, not all soldiers tasked with this duty had the best of handwriting. This was often aggravated by emergency situations that were called in, such as an aircraft being shot down, or someone wounded or killed. For instance, if a Mayday was called in, the voice of the pilot sending the message was often strained to a much higher octave than normal. For the most part, we all recognized each other's voices. When it sounded like the person calling in a Mayday or severe hit report had his undies in a severe bind, it often made for a stressful situation for the guys back in Operations. The clerk was not only responsible for writing a brief entry in the log, but he was also responsible for knowing whom to notify. There were entries that were simple facts stated. When at other times, he had to notify Battalion, call for more helicopters to insert additional troops (called the Blue Team, or Blues), call for gunship support, flare bird support and/or fighter support.

I have inserted original copies of some of these reports to give you a feel for what I'm writing about. I have then interpreted parts of the reports that may be difficult to understand. In some cases, it's difficult to decipher what was written. When the Company gets into a serious firefight, you can be assured that events get pretty dicey and that the radio stays hot with excited conversation. It's at times like this when an otherwise slow day picks up to a feverish pitch. It's also a time when the Duty Officer or lowly SP4 Clerk gets a sweaty workout. When he finds out that a crewmember that is a personal friend has been shot down, severely injured, or killed, it makes for tough duty often hidden behind tears of grief.

				PAGE NO. 1	NO. OF PAGES 3

DAILY STAFF JOURNAL OR DUTY OFFICER'S LOG

DECLASSIFIED
Authority NND873541
By [W] NARA Date 5/22/12

ORGANIZATION OR INSTALLATION	LOCAT	PERIOD COVERED	

FROM		TO	
HOUR	DATE 19 APRIL	HOUR 2400	DATE 19 APRIL

ITEM NO.	TIME IN	TIME OUT	INCIDENTS, MESSAGES, ORDERS, ETC.	ACTION TAKEN	INITIALS
1	0500		0600 m/R Report 3925	Called ND 65	DEB
2	0555		Called 3 about sending out birds LRRP	Called Companies	
	0605		mission Weather. All missions are on	~ ND 65	DEB
			weather Hotel		
3	0830		PM Y-2 CRASHED IN LZ ON LRRP INSERTION AWAITING FURTHER DETAILS	PASSED TO ND65	DEK
4	0850		RECEIVED WORD RECOVERY BIRD ON WAY TO LOCATION. CREW OK. 2 PAX WITH INJURY. 1 - BROKEN LEG + 1 INTERNAL DAMAGE		
5	0855		RECEIVED WORD ANOTHER A/C DOWN (NEGATIVE ASSESSMENT W-?)		
6	0856	ND65	RECEIVED WORD BIRD IS RETURNING DUE TO EXCESSIVE VIBRATION. DID NOT GO DOWN	PASSED TO 5 + 3 4	DEK
7	0900	PMY-1	SAID MED-EVAC w/PENETROTOR WAS AFFECTING RECOVERY OF LWAS ON PMY-2. IF CREW COULD NOT BE EXTRACTED ON NEXT PASS PM FLIGHT WOULD EXTRACT THEM. WAS NOT SHOT DOWN		OK
8	0910	B-CO	RECEIVED WORD THAT PM Y-2 WAS SHOT DOWN. TRYING TO GET CONFIRMATION		DEK
9	0924	ND65	GREEN 2 SHOT DOWN. NOTHING LEFT OF SHIP. TROOPS WERE ON BOARD		DEK
10	0930		WSC at this location w/High frequency		DCC
11	0940		WHITE 7 Returning for excessive Vibration C Has NOT ARRIVED AS OF 1000.		AAR
12	1010	ND65	RECEIVED WORD THAT Fox + Ammo PENTIGI		DCC
13	1010		PULLED Two BIRDS FROM LEFT RXF TO RIGHT BIRDS IN ORANGE SIGHT ALSO 1 c/s from 229th.		DCC
14	1030	C-8	RECEIVED SOI + GUNS FROM DOWNED AC of LAST NIGHT GROUP	PASSED ON TO GROUP	DEK
15	1040	C-Co	Y-5 DOWN w/NEAR STRIKE VC DOWN TREES		DCR

TYPED NAME AND SIGNATURE OF OFFICER OR OFFICIAL ON DUTY	SIGNATURE
	Downgraded at 3 year intervals Declassified after 12 years

CONFIDENTIAL

DA FORM 1594
1 NOV 62

PREVIOUS EDITION OF THIS FORM IS OBSOLETE.

DAILY STAFF JOURNAL OR DUTY OFFICER'S LOG (AR 22)				PAGE NO. 2	NO OF PAGES 3

DECLASSIFIED
Authority NND883541
By W NARA Date 5/22/02

ORGANIZATION OR INSTALLATION		LOCATION	PERIOD COVERED		
			FROM		TO
			DATE 19APR68	HOUR 2400	DATE 19APR68

ITEM NO.	TIME IN	TIME OUT	INCIDENTS, MESSAGES, ORDERS, ETC.	ACTION TAKEN	INITIALS
16	1045		RECEIVED WORD THAT W2 IS OK & STILL FLYING		DCK
17	1050	KC65	KC 37 WENT DOWN. CREW INBOUND. NEG-	PASSED TO WJ6,5,3,34	
			ATIVE FURTHER ON STATUS OF SHIP		DCK
18	1115	KC9	KC 37 (108) RECEIVED ROUNDS IN ROCKET		
			PODS + FUEL CELL. SHIP WAS AFIRE +	PASSED TO	
			SET DOWN. CREW OK	WJ5,34,34,W065	DCK
19	1125	WD65	SINGLE SHIPS NOT USING FLIGHT FOLLOWING	PASSED TO A&CO	
			ADVISED TO DO SO.	WJSM	DCK
20	1200		BLACK BANDIT 555 REPORTED.		WJ
			WILL JOIN THE WHITE FLIGHT		
21	1210	A CO	RECEIVED HIT REPORT.	PASSED TO DANGER 65	WJ
22	1213	—	PASSED ON TO A CO THAT		WJ
			AS SOON AS A BIRD COMES		
			UP, IT WILL JOIN THE B CO		
			BIRD ON LRRP INS.		
23	1235	WD2	REQUIRE ALL HIT REPORTS BY TOD. ALSO	PASSED TO WJ3	
			ALL MAINT + ACCIDENT FAILURES		DCK
24	1245	A Co	DS24 A/c 719 TO RTT TO LRRP MOVE	PASSED TO WD65	DCK
25	1300	WD65	HRL 1225, YD303129 SOCAL GUN POSITION	PASSED TO WJ6,5,3	DCK
26	1310		PASSED HIT REPORT TO SKY-		WJ
			ROCKET 2		
27	1315	WD65	RECEIVED WORD TO HAVE FLS CTR FLASHING JADER ON THEIR UHF. WILL ADVISE BEST ROUTES TO LZ. HAVE KNOWLEDGE OF ENEMY GUN POSITIONS	PASSED TO WJ6,3	DCK

TYPED NAME AND GRADE OF OFFICER OR OFFICIAL ON DUTY	SIGNATURE

DA FORM 1594 PREVIOUS EDITION OF THIS FORM IS OBSOLETE.

ITEM:

2. Called Three about sending out a Long Range Recon Patrol mission. All flights postponed due to weather.

3. Yellow Two crashed in LZ on LRRP insertion. Awaiting further details.

4. A recovery aircraft is on the way to Yellow Two location. Crew OK. Two passengers injured. One broken leg, one internal injuries.

5. Another bird down. No assessment.

6. Another ship returning to base with excessive vibration. Did not go down. (In a helicopter, any vibrations are suspected problems and could quickly lead to catastrophic failure. There are many moving parts on a chopper, and they must operate smoothly for a safe flight).

7. Medevac with jungle penetrator was helping with recovery of WIAs. If crew could not be extracted, an afternoon flight would extract them. Was not shot down. (As you can tell by now, due to poor radio contact or confusion and stress, the reports were not always accurate...much like the news reports we listen to today.

8. Yellow Two was shot down. Trying to get confirmation.

9. Green Two shot down. Ship destroyed. Troops on board.

14. Retrieved passengers and guns from last night's crash.

15. Yellow Five down with rotor blade strike. Probably hit tree. Yellow Six down with transmission problems.

16. White Seven is OK and still flyable.

17. KC37 aircraft went down. Crew is inbound. No more info on status of aircraft.

18. KC37 received enemy rounds in rocket pods and fuel cell. Ship was on fire and landed somewhere. Crew OK.

19. Single ships not using flight following. Advised to do so. When an aircraft is on a mission, they are supposed to call in their position periodically to either Operations or to another aircraft that can relay the info. If they crash, a last position and time is known to affect a search.

23. Operations require all enemy fire, accident and maintenance reports be turned in by 5 pm.
25. Hill 1225, coordinates Y) 303129 has an enemy .50 cal. gun position.
26. Passed hit report to Skyrocket Two.
27. Flights are to contact Flashing Saber on their UHF radio to ask for advice on best routes to fly to designated LZ. He has knowledge of enemy gun positions.
28. Another chopper is down. Crew OK. Status and cause not available.
30. Huey hit tree or stump. Overturned and is on fire. Crew OK.
33. . 50 cal. positions with coordinates. Numerous NVA troops moving north of the road at grid coordinate 2908.
34. Flare ship called out for mission.

CHAPTER 4

William E. Peterson

Shaken Man

Satisfying his hunger pangs after having spent the past 6 weeks in the bush, a guy who appears as though he eats rocks for lunch, leaves the mess tent with a tremendous belch. Gerry Armstrong, Point Man with Bravo, 1/9th Cav is on a two day stand-down at Camp Evans after spending several weeks patrolling the boonies west of Evans where his company has been engaged in several heavy firefights.

They've had seven buddies killed during this time. Thirteen more men have been wounded by the North Vietnamese Army. Out of the thirteen WIA, four will likely come back to the unit after they've been patched up by the nearest field hospital. Their wounds were not critical. However, the other nine all had wounds that are often called "Million Dollar Wounds"–meaning their horrible tours in Viet Nam have ended. For most of these young men, that's a good thing. To have to deal with the life threatening and life altering nature of their wounds is an entirely different story.

Lying awake in a hospital bed in excruciating pain while thinking of what their family members, wife, girlfriend and other loved ones will think when they hear the horrible news, adds a tremendous amount of stress. Mind-boggling questions have been the norm for each of these young men ever since they arrived in country. When

21

most of us landed on Vietnamese soil, we had heard so many horror stories that we all wondered if we would return to America wounded, dead, or not at all. After a short while, most of us realized these stories weren't fiction.

One of the KIA's was Gerry's best friend, Kyle Marker, from his hometown. They had joined the Army on the buddy system and had managed to stay together through Basic and Infantry training. Arriving in Viet Nam together, they were assigned to the same company and had fought side by side for the past seven months. An enemy machine gun has ripped Kyle to pieces while Gerry, by his side, emptied a full magazine from his M16 on the machine gunner. It was too late to save his childhood buddy.

Gerry's unit choppered in just before dark last evening, a hot shower, a clean set of fresh jungle cammies, and hot chow at the "all you can eat" mess tent have changed Gerry's outlook on life substantially. When he arrived last evening, he looked like something out of a horror movie. Other than rinsing off in the many forded rivers over the past deployment to the boonies, bathing has not been on the agenda. His normal dimpled smile and good looks have been traded for a deep tan, scraggly hair and beard, heavy bags under his eyes, and a distant haunting, kind of spooky look. Cuts and bruises from hiking and sometimes crawling through the jungle are covered with encrusted blood and mud. His blood-saturated clothing is soaked from helping his fellow wounded and dying soldiers in the recent firefights. He's covered with mud and jungle debris that has attached itself to the sticky life-blood of the young men who were either dying, or had already sacrificed their lives in an attempt to not only save themselves, but who have courageously fought to keep their buddies alive. His shredded fatigues flap when he walks. It's no wonder Gerry's smile is non-existent, he's been through hell and knew that all he could look forward to was more of the same for another five months, before he would have a ticket for that "Freedom Bird" back to his home, family, friends, and that very special blonde-headed gal, Jessie, who he loved so dearly.

The initial assault into the enemy infested A Shau Valley is planned for first light tomorrow. By all intelligence reports, this assault will be one of the bloodiest of the war, and we'll probably suffer a lot of casualties. With these thoughts going through his mind and silently wondering if he will be sent home in a body bag, it's time to find a quiet place to sit down and write to his parents. Finding a shady place on a pile of sandbags next to the maintenance tent, Gerry writes:

Dear Mom and Dad,

Having just arrived at Camp Evans for a couple of days of down time, my mail has finally caught up to me. I have a letter from Tammie (sister) telling me of her dating escapades. Her letters are always so uplifting with her great sense of humor. I just wish I could be there to supervise her dates.

I was saddened to hear of Granny's passing. She was such a special lady and I have many fond memories of spending the better part of my summers at the farm with her and Pa.

I've been out in the field for the past six weeks or so. Though the countryside is breathtaking, this camping out is getting old. It has sure been nice to be able to be near Kyle for the past several months. We were so fortunate to have been assigned to the same unit.

I'll have to admit to having been very shaken in the last few days. I have some very sad news. Our company was engaged in a heavy firefight three days ago. Fifteen minutes into the attack, Kyle and I were fighting shoulder-to-shoulder when an enemy machine-gunner opened up on our unit. I was taken by complete surprise when Kyle disappeared from my peripheral view. I knew he had been hit hard, and I immediately took the enemy gunner out. I knelt down by my life-long friend and tried desperately to bring him back to life. The firefight continued for another thirty minutes or so. When the firing stopped, I sat down and held Kyle's bloodied and now lifeless body in my arms for several minutes while the floodgates opened. I could not hold back my tears for my lost hero. I cried out to God, "Why did you have to take my best friend away from me?" I am so glad Kyle was a Christian. I'll see him again in a much better place than this hell hole. His family will undoubtedly have been notified of this tragedy by the time you get this. Please tell them how sorry I am that I was unable to protect their fine son. I feel responsible, even though I know I had no control over this horrible tragedy.

The Cav is going on a major assault in the morning into the A Shau Valley. That's where I'll be for the next week or so. I'm sure it will be a piece of cake, so please don't worry about me.

I love all of you,
Gerry

At 1900 Captain Thurmond calls our company together to introduce the "Cherries" (new men) who have been assigned to us to replace those men lost on our last venture. We have only five replacements: Ray Jones from Valparaiso, Texas, BJ Robbins from Milwaukee, Wisconsin, Mac Sousa from San Bernardino, California, Jimmie Ramirez from Chama, New Mexico, and Don Feldson from Olathe, Kansas. In their non-faded jungle fatigues, un-marred boots, white complexions, and young, innocent appearance, these guys look scary to all of us. Though we all fit their boots months prior when we first came into the country, we realize all the mistakes we made as "newbies". Yet, we are responsible for training these guys and getting them up to speed so they can fight confidently alongside of us, it's always difficult to make friends with new guys. They often make fatal mistakes before they're properly trained. We don't want to lose more friends.

Sleeping restlessly through the incoming enemy mortars and outgoing Cav artillery, Gerry spends a lot of time wondering what his fate might be in the morning on yet another flight into hell.

CHAPTER 5

William E. Peterson

Invincible

Every time we have a mission to pick up a load of grunts, I wonder what goes through their minds during their pre-mission briefing. They often get their briefings just prior to our arrival to take them into battle.

When they're told what to expect in the area of operations, the information given is generally from gathered "intelligence". Occasionally that is exactly what they experience, but all too often the available info is old, sketchy, or even non-existent. When they're told to expect a cold LZ, it may be hot – very hot! Conversely, when they're expecting a hot LZ, they get extremely psyched up, and some can't wait to tear into the enemy. Others, some old timers, and other new guys are as scared as they have ever been in their lives. In reality, they're all scared. Some just don't want to admit it.

The old timer may be scared because he's been in the "green" almost a year. This may be his last week, last day, or last mission in the boonies. In actuality, this minute could be his last on this earth! He may have a sweetheart waiting for him – or at least that's what she promised in her last letter. He may be wondering if his girl, or wife, has been true to him while he's been gone all these hot, sweaty, cold and wet, extremely dangerous, horrifying, grueling, scary, almost always bloody days. There's way too much talk about it amongst his buddies, so a guy can't help but have intrusive thoughts. Intrusive thoughts can kill you here in 'Nam. It can kill you slowly from the inside and absolutely eat your guts out. Or, not paying full attention while in the boonies, a bullet or booby trap can kill you very quickly.

Daydreaming about his girl when the aircraft touches down in the LZ, he charges out of the helicopter, obviously not thinking straight. He's dodging enemy bullets and mortars, RPGs, grenades and booby traps, and returning fire while he runs for cover. He's trying to keep the nasty red dirt and debris out of his eyes, nose and throat that's swirling all around him from the choppers in the hot LZ. His adrenaline is pumping faster than he's ever experienced. Subconsciously he wonders what's happening, thinking he could die here on the LZ with all this commotion, when...he runs into a helicopter tail rotor. Unfortunately, that has happened numerous times.

He's scared because he wonders if he may be blown out of the sky on this mission. Granted, he has managed to stay alive this long. He or his buddies may have been wounded – possibly several times. Will he make it home to see his wife and children while still alive, or will his family be cremating what's left of his body when he returns lifeless, if he returns at all? Sometimes, remains are never found. What if he's captured on this mission and becomes a P.O.W. for the next several years, for the rest of his life, or until he's tortured to death?

Some of the guys, who've been here awhile, never get used to combat assaults, and understandably have great disgust for them. The new young men have little or no idea what to expect, and the fear of the unknown causes them to question themselves. How will I stand up in combat? Will I be able to kill the enemy? Even though I was trained to kill the enemy, I certainly wasn't raised that way. How will I feel after shooting another soldier? Will I be paralyzed at the very thought?

If they've already pulled a tour in Viet Nam, their lives have already changed. They've seen combat firsthand, been through the forge, hammered and toughened beyond belief. Either they're Lifers, planning on making a career of the military, and their number has come up again to serve another tour, or they enjoy the adrenaline rush, or the killing so much, they've come back for more. Often these men either think they're invincible, or believe they're not going to make it back to their loved ones anyway. So, why not enjoy life for a few more hours, minutes or perhaps… seconds. I have personally experienced this.

We're not playing war in the neighbor's barn with BB guns anymore. This is a deadly game. If these young men have been on many assaults, they know what's coming and it's never pretty.

I'm beginning to feel guilty every time we do a combat assault knowing beforehand that several of the men we take into the depths of enemy territory, may not return unscathed. Not only that, they may not return at all.

It tears my heart out every time we fly medevac missions. That's not the normal protocol for our Company. However, the medevac units are often short of aircraft, so we willingly fill in whenever possible. These men need helicopter assistance NOW!

During their ride in our helicopter, or another, their eyes may not reflect the fear that's evident among most during an air assault. Instead, on their next ride out of the jungle, their eyes may be closed – inside a body bag. All too frequently, there are so many dead men for us to pick up, that there aren't enough body bags. When this happens, their eyes are all too visible while they lie on the deck of the ship, that final distant look staring blankly into what lies beyond.

Regardless, every man who joins us on a helicopter assault will never be the same. Combat changes one – forever.

CHAPTER 6

William E. Peterson

Valley Of Death

Following the briefing last evening, there was a lot of speculation amongst the crews as we discussed tomorrow's mission into the dreaded A Shau Valley. According to all intelligence reports, the A Shau has always been an enemy stronghold and is secluded in between mountains about a twenty-minute flight to the west of Camp Evans. It is home to a lot of inclement weather for the majority of the year. The next week or two is a window that the weather guys are forecasting to be suitable for not only our initial assault, but also for flight support. Without decent weather to allow our choppers to continue flying missions for the duration of the engagement, our LZ's could quickly be overrun without the necessary ammo, weapons, water, and food. Not to mention the many medevac missions that are foreseen in the battle we're about to begin.

With so much negative speculation, I decide to hit the rack early and get plenty of rest for a grueling day of battle. Sporadic incoming mortars throughout the night, even though not in the near vicinity of where I'm attempting to sleep, keep me on edge. They aren't close enough to cause me to head for our nearby bunker until 0115 when three rounds hit almost simultaneously within seventy-five yards or so of our crew chief tent. We all grab our weapons and dive into our bunker where we stay for thirty minutes until the gooks decide to call it a night.

When the rest of the guys go back to bed, I put my boots on, grab my weapon and go for a walk around the company area in an attempt to shake off the demons that are haunting me. Walking past three tents, I run into one of our guards who is armed with a loaded .12 gauge and very alert due to the incoming we've had.

"Halt, who goes there?"

I know, sounds weird, but that's the standard call the guard is supposed to make to see if I am friend or foe. I answer with the password, "Pittsburgh," (at least that's what I thought it was). I have it right and have a friendly chat with Charlie. He's one of our gunners who stretches out at six-foot, three inches. All I can see are the whites of his eyes. His dark skin blends in with the coal-black night.

The NVA use darkness to their advantage. I swear they can see like cats. It would be a great night for them to attempt to overwhelm us with a ground attack.

Deciding this is probably not a good time for a walk in the park, I go back to my cot and flop down for more dramatized thoughts of what the A Shau Valley might bring. Drifting off to a fitful sleep, horrible visions pass in review. I see chopper loads of body bags being flown back to camp and am praying I am not looking at one from the inside. I can see the inside of my aircraft splattered with blood and guts, flaming choppers hit by anti-aircraft and .50 cal fire. My mind conjures up radio calls from the grunts on the ground; their now high-pitched sounding voices are crying out for air support.

"We're being overrun from all sides."

"We need medevac ASAP! Three men critical!"

"Drop your napalm on the west side of LZ Pepper...DANGER CLOSE!"

"God help us!"

As air support is supplied to the endangered troops, more cries of Mayday are heard:

"Mayday, Mayday, Mayday Bandit One Two hit. heading east at 2200 feet."

"Mayday, Mayday, Mayday Viper One Niner going down one mile north of Pepper."

"Mayday, Mayday, Mayday Little Bear Two One...We've lost hydraulics!"

There are a lot of reported anti-aircraft positions in the area where our missions will take place. If I'm shot down again, I hope we don't have a load of grunts...our very special passengers. That would make it a joyful day for Charlie. We certainly don't want the enemy to be happy. I'm having a tough time shaking the horrendous thoughts.

As usual, our local artillery battery fires rounds all night in an attempt to knock out the enemy mortar fire. Additionally, as requests are made from units in the field, firing missions are sent out to relieve the ground pounders. I've been in country long enough to distinguish incoming from outgoing fire, but the concern over the upcoming mission keeps me awake until 0430 when the Orderly, Larry Lizotte (affectionately known as "Lizzard"), saunters into our tent to wake us. He doesn't have to be selective this morning about which crews he awakens. We're all needed to make the initial assault on the A Shau Valley, "The Valley of Death".

None of us have slept well, knowing what dangers and likely bloodshed will greet us this morning.

Since I'm already dressed from my short walk, I go to the nearby lister bag, brush my teeth, fill my steel pot (helmet) with warm water from the immersion tank, and do a quick GI bath. A devilish thought crosses my mind; it feels weird to be washing a body that may soon be consumed in a fiery crash. Looking to the east, I see the faint morning glow. Will today be my day? Am I ready to die? A spooky thought.

Oh dear God...Please clear my mind. I'm counting on your divine protection throughout this day.

It's almost 0600 hours when I gather up my flight gear and head for Flight Ops. Opening the tent flap, the smell of that awful coffee from our nasty coffee pot, and cloud of cigarette, cigar, and pipe smoke make me want to vomit. After more speculation amongst the crews, Major Stevens enters the tent while sucking on his ever-present stub of a cigar.

30

"Gentlemen...as you know all too well, yesterday was a tough day. Today will likely be worse. Due to weather restrictions over the past several months, there have been no Americans in the A Shau Valley for a long while. Intelligence tells us to expect heavy resistance. We expect the presence of major supply depots, hospitals, training, and staging areas. Men, this is where the Ho Chi Minh trail turns into a superhighway."

Looking around the tent full of aircrews, I wonder whom the Major is talking to when he refers to us as "gentlemen" and "men". Actually, some of our guys aren't even shaving yet. The majority of us are only eighteen or nineteen. If the thoughts I have had regarding this mission are close to correct, we are about to age considerably.

"The next few weeks are the transition period between the two monsoons, when the valley has a break from the incessant rains and cloud cover. Numerous anti-aircraft batteries are expected throughout the valley. Those weapons include: 37mm and 23mm guns, and 12.7mm, 14.5mm, and .50 cal machine guns. There are reported to be several regiments in the area, including armored elements and possibly fixed-wing and helicopter battalions.

"Looking at the map over here, you can see that the known sites for enemy anti-aircraft and .50 cal have been marked. Be sure to copy these onto your charts. These are last known enemy positions, but reports are that there are likely a lot more that have yet to be pinpointed. We'll be assaulting two LZs...LZ Tiger and LZ Pepper. More LZs will be established as the fighting continues. The enemy supply routes are well camouflaged. In some cases, the tops of trees have been bent over and woven together, hiding the trails."

And exactly why is it that we're going into "The Valley of Death", Major?

During the briefing by the Old Man, my feelings resurface when all the known gun positions are pointed out on the chart. There are so many marked that it will be tough to avoid them all. Even though I've flown through a lot of anti-aircraft and .50 caliber fire before, my premonitions make my skin crawl.

How can I be foolish enough to volunteer to fly into such a well-fortified valley? I must be crazy! Do I really think God will protect me through all of this?

We're a team...I can't let my buddies down. I will fulfill my duties as crew chief and gunner. I feel good about my final decision, because I've fought alongside most of these men for months, and we've always done everything in our power to help anyone in trouble. I couldn't ask for a better team of soldiers to fight alongside of me. I am blessed.

The camaraderie this morning seems especially strong. However, looking around the briefing tent and into the eyes of the rest of the crews, I can read their minds. They're all as terrified as I am. Will we be able to perform at our peak if we're this scared? On this mission, we must all be at the top of our game. Being scared is part of that.

"Men, I know I haven't painted a very pretty picture. I'm only giving you facts from the intelligence reports. This is extremely rugged country. Right now it belongs to Charles. By this afternoon, it'll be ours! Best of luck to each of you."

II Samuel 22: 5-7

5. The waves of death swirled about me; the torrents of destruction overwhelmed me.

6. The cords of the grave coiled around me; the snares of death confronted me. 7. In my distress I called to the Lord; I called out to my God.

I pray for God to remove those snares of death and protect us all on the flight today. However, I really don't feel like I'm praying with a lot of faith.

CHAPTER 7

William E. Peterson

A Shau Valley

19 April, 1968
Camp Evans

In order to fly in combat, cocky crews are almost always the norm. It's not that we think we're invincible. We've seen so many buddies killed in this business; we're firm believers that instant death can and does come when you least expect it. I don't think we have death wishes either. Maybe it's a defense mechanism. From my very first mission to this day, I don't think I'll make it home alive. For months that thought spooked me in the worst way. Today, for some reason, I feel like I'm ready to face death, and accept it for what it is. But in retrospect, I would sure like to make it home in one piece. I don't want to miss out on any more hunting and fishing. And, I think I want to marry Cindi.

Following the briefing, the cocky edge has worn down on all of us. Walking up the trail to the flight line following the briefing, I'm pondering what will be inscribed on my tombstone. Thoughts of a battle with death continue to haunt me. God will have His hands full today, but I'm confident He can handle it.

And yet, I am sorely lacking in faith this morning.

When the briefing is complete, the flight crews exit the tent as if

33

they're leaving a funeral parlor. Rather than the normal noisy cockiness that has been so prevalent prior to most missions, there is total silence while we each wrestle with the thoughts passing through our minds.

On the way to the flight line Eddie and I make small talk, but the extreme danger of the upcoming mission makes deep conversation impossible.

We're going to hit Charlie hard today with forty slicks each loaded down with 6-7 psyched up grunts. This is just the initial insertion at daybreak. The plan is to continue flying more men and equipment into the "Valley of Death" all day. The mission...to overwhelm Charlie and hit him where it really puts a bind on him. We'll have a heavy compliment of gunships including B model Hueys and cobras. There will also be plenty of TAC air and artillery supporting the mission. A couple of slicks with only flight crews are going to accompany the flight, their sole purpose...search and rescue...*a very humbling thought.*

Arriving at the revetment where my ship 092 has spent the night, I'm reminded about all the missions this aircraft has brought me safely through. Seeing the many familiar bullet-hole patches that I've completed since she was brand new, she stands proud in the pale early morning light. I can only hope and pray that she will do the same today.

Eddie busies himself with mounting the machine guns, loading the ammo trays, and hanging smoke, frags, and incendiary grenades in all the usual places by each of our seats while I do the preflight. "Chief" (Eddie, a Choctaw Indian) is thankfully a fierce fighter, the best gunner in our outfit, in my opinion. He always takes a lot of extra "arrows" to the fight. We're very close buddies, and have successfully fought many battles together. This one looks like it will be the biggest fight to date. We're both on edge, ready to go off. I guess that's a good thing; we're well prepared to be successful on today's battlefield.

All appears normal and the bird is ready to fly. After I top off the engine oil reservoir, the pilots show up with their armloads of flight gear. Mr. Jewitt is our Aircraft Commander today, and for that I'm grateful. He and I have flown many missions together. He's one of my favorite Charlie company pilots, very competent with a good sense of humor and a great friend. Mr. Clark, also an excellent pilot will be the co-pilot today. And, of course, Eddie will be my very capable gunner.

How can things go wrong with such a qualified crew?

Mr. Clark does his pre-flight to double check my work. Two sets of eyes are certainly better than one and we always like to find any problems while still on the ground. After checking the aircraft logbook for any previous write-ups by other pilots, the crew chief or maintenance crews, he signs the aircraft off for flight...into the unknown.

According to the briefing, there will be forty slicks involved in the initial insertion, just after daybreak. We'll have a heavy compliment of gunships including B model Hueys and cobras. There will also be plenty of TAC air and artillery supporting the mission. And, as usual on a mission of this size...search and rescue aircraft. There are a lot of soldiers involved today, all putting our lives on the line. Though today's mission into the teeth of the enemy is necessary to break the backs of the NVA, it will prove to be very costly to us all...either physically...or mentally. We'll never forget what is about to take place.

The slot assigned to 092 today is Yellow Five. That means that my ship will be the fifth aircraft to land in the LZ.

At the appointed time of 0645 hours Yellow One turns on the anti-collision light and cranks our warbird. Slowly the main rotor and tail rotor blades begin to stir, soon swirling the air and red clay dust into an eerie looking mixture amidst the early morning light and red flashing beacon.

When Yellow One checks in on the radio, he calls each of the other Aircraft Commanders individually to be sure they're all in contact and ready to go. In fairly close unison, the balance of the choppers posted in various places on the flight line join in with their own dust storm. With all the combined rotor wash, flashing red beacons, dawn and light fog, this scene is surreal.

When all are accounted for and a clearance is received from the tower, the flight departs the helicopter revetment parking area to reposition on the Camp Evans airstrip where the grunts are waiting in anticipation. The infantrymen are very well organized and clustered in small groups along the edge of the airstrip, many of them having done this dozens of times before. The new guys just follow the old timers. Most are fearful of the unknown. Some don't realize what there is to be afraid of, but they'll soon get a first hand account of genuine fear. When all aircraft are loaded, the flight joins up in formation just outside the western edge of the perimeter. The orange ball on the eastern horizon confirms that we're on time. We're headed for LZs Tiger and Pepper.

No one is specifically assigned to help the new soldiers. They're expected to mimic the war heroes that have come before them. If the experienced troopers have lived for any length of time in this God-forsaken mess, they're very knowledgeable on surviving in a war zone. Too many of us have lost buddies that we have become very close to. The tendency after that happens in Viet Nam is to not make any more close friends. They become statistics too easily, and the new men often don't make it through their early days without good mentors. Some are killed on their first mission. I pray that won't happen today.

Departing due west, our flight of 1st Cav choppers is poised to strike the enemy where he's hiding out in the mountainous jungles and lush valleys of northwestern South Viet Nam.

Just after our gaggle forms up, Yellow One contacts the FAC pilot flying his O1 Bird Dog in the area we're to attack.

The FAC (Bird Dog pilot), sounding very perky and alert, announces that the mountains we're to cross on the east side of the A Shau Valley are shrouded in dense fog. He gives Yellow One the coordinates for a large rice paddy just east of the mountains where we can land our birds while waiting for the fog to lift. He's been circling over that area for the past several minutes and hasn't drawn any fire or seen anything out of the ordinary. He declares it a cold LZ.

The job of the FAC is to spot targets for the artillery, and fly low and slow to see if they can draw out any untrained enemy soldier that hasn't been taught to hold his fire and not shoot the little bird. It's really a decoy. Bird Dogs can't help but fly slow. They're a great, small, tandem aircraft, even though a bit squirrelly on landing. Top speed is about 110 knots.

Arriving over the dry rice paddy, our flight circles to the west to make its approach to the east. All eyes are on the ground searching for any telltale traces of enemy. All appears normal and peaceful. The beautiful jade green jungles covering the steep mountainsides are breath taking, especially with the wisps of scattered fog. Our compliment of gunships is doing its job flying alongside of the flight, searching for targets of opportunity. They're always hungry for a hot target. The entire flight spreads out over the full length and width of the LZ and lands like a gaggle of geese arriving in a harvested cornfield for breakfast.

Yellow One commands the flight to shut down to wait out the fog shrouding the mountains that we need to cross in order to get to the mountainous valley. The turbines wind down and the rotor blades slow. The flight crews and grunts depart the aircraft and mingle with their buddies talking about the mission with great nervousness and anticipation. Even though we've only been in the air twenty minutes, it will likely be a very long, unnerving day.

We're all grateful for the fog. Having to scrub the mission for thirty minutes or possibly an hour gives us the opportunity to walk around and shrug off some of our uneasiness. Talking with the grunts, it becomes obvious that their fear of today's mission is as great or greater than that of the flight crews. Last minute adjustments are made to equipment, each man checking the other, while we all wait on Mother Nature. I notice that even though our wait for the fog could take an hour or so, no one is sitting down. I guess we're all too hyped up to relax that much. Many of us are taking advantage of the scene and shooting photos. I climb up on my ship to take in the view, and use my camera to shoot some fantastic shots...the best shot is on the cover of my first book, *Missions Of Fire And Mercy~Until Death Do Us Part.*

(www.missionsoffireandmercy.com)

After twenty minutes on the ground, a look to the west reveals that the fog is beginning to lift. The decision is made by Yellow One to give the weather a few more minutes to be sure the flight path is clear.

A familiar muffled hissing sound is heard...

"INCOMING!!!"

We've obviously landed near the enemy, and he's targeting our LZ! The first mortar rounds land a safe distance from the ships, but as more rounds are fired, they're walking closer. The enemy has a forward observer hiding in the bushes, probably on a nearby ridge with a radio. He calls in the hits for the mortar crews and instructs them on the adjustments they need to make to score hits on the choppers sitting in the field.

All crews and their passengers run for the aircraft, crank, and take off to the east. The enemy fire continues as the last ship departs. Gunships rain fire on the adjacent tree line where the enemy mortar tubes are suspected. Miraculously, none of the aircraft or men is hit. It's sweet revenge when the enemy expends so many of their valuable rounds carried all the way from North Viet Nam and is only able to bag piles of mud! You can bet they're extremely disappointed and being chewed out by their Commander. Tickles me to death! OK, I guess that's the wrong word to use today.

By now, the sun has burned the fog off the tops of the mountains allowing us to continue our mission. Heading back to the west, we're only seven or eight minutes out from the two mountaintops that will serve as our LZs. Continuing to our destination at tree top level, we're avoiding the artillery prep that is being directed toward our targets by staying down low. The rounds are being fired from a couple of firebases and are whistling through the air above our flight. The grunts fidget with their gear. Nerves are taut while we anticipate the fate that lies ahead. All gunners recheck their machine guns, itchy fingers ready to deal death on the enemy.

Yellow One talks with the FAC on the radio. He's circling outside the line of the artillery fire. Between transmissions, he's talking with Six, circling high over the valley in his Charlie-Charlie ship awaiting our arrival. The task for Six will be to direct the concert below on the radios. The "music" will likely be very loud!

Approaching the base of the mountains, we see the plumes of black smoke from the artillery barrage. When we see a white plume of smoke, it's from a "Willy Peter" (white phosphorous artillery round) and signals that the artillery batteries will now discontinue firing, so our flight is safe from being hit by an artillery round.

We're all grateful for the proficient artillery battery crews. They not only prep our LZs, but provide fire when called upon for units that are under attack. They're deadly, and usually right on target.

The birds in the front of the formation begin to take small arms and automatic weapons fire while the accompanying gunships spray the area with mini-gun fire. The confusion of so many pilots calling in enemy locations, the voice of FAC, the Artillery Prep Commander and Six, plus the loud voices of the grunts getting psyched up is mind-boggling. The voices of the warriors ready to continue the fight on the ground are heard over the horrendous sounds of battle. My adrenaline is flowing to the max. When I first started flying missions, it was all but impossible to separate all the different voices and what was being said over more than one frequency; but after flying hundreds of similar missions, I'm now able to understand the majority of the radio transmissions. During such an involved flight over the battlefield, flight plans must be changed with split-second decisions. It can become even more chaotic and dramatic very quickly.

Flight Leader, Yellow One talks to the FAC again for any late reports on the enemy. He's also talking with Six, circling high over the valley in his "Charlie-Charlie" ship awaiting our arrival.

The well-orchestrated symphony will likely start out like all of our attack concerts, a rapid rendition with the snare drums, an ever increasing roll from the kettle drums, several reverberating booms from the base drum, and followed by a clashing of the symbols like tyrants. The trumpets sound the attack, while the tuba rains down gunship rocket fire. The snare drums send out their rapid staccato from the mini-guns and M60 machine guns. The conductor has already stained his seasoned tuxedo with salty sweat that's now running down his face. Something has gone terribly wrong – rather than audience applause, the musicians are receiving gunfire from all quadrants. The director wants nothing more than his well-oiled orchestra to be able to pack up their instruments and dive for a foxhole.

Flying closer to our assigned LZs, the crescendo of fire increases to a volume like none other. Willy Pete has hit the ground at each LZ signaling that the last artillery rounds have left the tubes and we're at least safe from that hazard. But another danger takes its place...we're taking on .50 cal. fire...and now, 37mm ack-ack (anti-aircraft fire) is leaving its black puffs of smoke amidst our flight. We can live with the smoke, but if we fly too close to it, the shrapnel within will eat our Hueys alive.

My heart feels like it's about to explode inside my chest! What have I gotten myself into? Will my premonition come true?

The gunships are doing a superb job of dusting off the anti-aircraft and .50 cal. sites with their tubes of rockets. At the same time, they're giving the lush jungle a good hosing with their miniguns and 20mm cannons. Without them, we'd all be toast. The combined sounds are destroying my hearing. We're all young and somewhat naïve soldiers. Yes, the flight crews are wearing helmets, but the hearing protection inside is pretty much worthless. None of us have been issued any kind of hearing protection, including the grunts. But, the thought of destroying our hearing doesn't really compute at our young ages. Thirty-five plus years later, the audiology lab at the VA is slammed with guys being fitted for hearing aids.

The pilots set up a high approach In order to clear the 150 foot triple canopy trees on all sides. This type of approach requires our choppers to come in not only high, but also slow in order to not overfly the small landing zone. If a pilot has to go around after a bad approach, his crew and passengers are exposed to even more enemy fire while it has to circle and fly a new approach. The aircraft in this case is lower and slower...a very bad place to be in this territory! These are tricky approaches for any helicopter pilot due to the ever-changing winds in the mountains, the varied terrain, the required precision, and the fact that this makes our birds extremely vulnerable to enemy gunners hiding in the shadows. We're all on edge, and if I may speak for all of us... we're scared spitless. After seeing my first approach like this, I always knew we were in the dead man's curve. That terminology is used in helicopter circles, meaning that when a chopper is low and slow, usually less than forty-five knots, and below 100 feet things can get dicey. In the event of an engine failure or a catastrophic failure of other critical aircraft components while in this flight mode, the chance of having enough time to enter a proper auto-rotation is real iffy. Even when the engine fails, if the conditions are right and the pilot well trained, he can enter an auto-rotation and land safely. If the conditions are as stated and the pilot is daydreaming, well...you can fill in the blank.

The LZ we're approaching looks extremely hazardous. The breathtaking emerald green triple canopy jungle at the top of this mountain has a gaping hole carved in it from B52 strikes that took place early this morning. The artillery prep ended just moments prior to our arrival. The shattered trees and grotesque looking stumps scattered about are surrounded by dense jungle on all sides. The ridgeline is very narrow, dropping off steeply for about 200 feet on either side. It's a very eerie looking site...soon to be a fiery grave.

The pinnacle approach and landing are a nightmare that I don't care to relive. But a Hand much more powerful than ours guides us to safely deposit our loads of valiant infantrymen.

Enemy resistance is light to moderate. Except for a few bullet and shrapnel holes, all forty ships escape unscathed to pick up a load of fuel, ammo and another load of men to reinforce those already engaged with the enemy at the LZs overlooking the A Shau Valley.

On the second insertion, our luck runs out. Even though we receive the usual small arms and automatic weapons fire, and have an occasional .50 cal. round slung at us, the AAA appears to be quiet. Making our approach to the same LZ where we did the first landing, the "pucker factor is still in the brown arc." The grunts on the ground are giving us cover fire to keep the gooks' heads down, as my gunner and I are hosing the area outside the perimeter with our 60s while leaning out the doors and watching for tree stumps that could abruptly end our flight. Our ship comes to a two-foot hover enabling the grunts to bail out. Staying at a hover enables us to make a faster exit than if we touch down. With bullets whizzing by and striking our ships, we want to get out as quickly as possible and want to make room for the aircraft that's about to come in right on our tail.

When the last man is about to jump from my aircraft, a burst of machine gun fire hits him in the chest and blows him back into our chopper. His blood splatters all over the ship and bathes both my gunner and I.

I quickly yell to the pilot,

"Sir, we have a severely wounded grunt on board who needs an immediate medevac."

"Rog, Pete."

That's the only reply I get. The pilots are super busy making the takeoff while we're drawing fire. Bullets are ripping through the skin of our ship, and Eddie and I are frantically returning fire. We're always determined to hit the enemy. Now more than ever, we're out for revenge for the mangled man lying on the floor of our ship.

Adding power, the pilot begins the takeoff while we're on the guns and watching for stumps. Suddenly...we find one...with the main rotor blades! The sound is horrendous while our expensive weed-whacker chews up the top of a tall stump. It sounds like a truck hitting the side of the mountain. Shards of wood and main rotor blades scatter across the LZ. The grunts on the ground are running for cover from the falling debris and the possibility of a helicopter crashing down on them. Mr. Jewitt hesitates slightly while grappling with the decision to either crash land in the LZ, outside of the LZ, into the hands of the enemy, or risk flying to a safer area. Crashing in the LZ will risk the lives of not only the crew, but also the lives of the grunts on the ground. If we crash here, it's likely we'll slide over the edge of either cliff. There would be no survivors. A departure with our severely damaged blades will probably not be a good choice. Adding the necessary pitch – and, therefore, stress – to the rotor system for flight will undoubtedly cause further damage and induce a fiery crash. It's a long shot, but Mr. Jewitt departs the LZ. We feel like we're inside a paint shaker; the vibrations are frightening! Split second decisions are an important makeup of an excellent pilot. The decision is made to try to clear the treetops and 092 did, thanks to the finesse of the man at the controls and the good Lord above. The aircraft is vibrating so badly I think she's going to shake herself to death. Mr. Clark has his hands close to the controls in the event that both pilots are needed to keep the bird from crashing.

Mr. Jewitt's voice is very shaky over the intercom due to the extreme vibrations of the chopper. Undoubtedly, a lot of the reason for the shaky voice is also due to his strong commitment to keep us all alive. That responsibility now lies with the skill of the Aircraft Commander – not to mention God's powerful hand over us. Actually, let's put God first here. We need all the help we can get!

The A.C. now asks in a very strained voice,

"Pete, do you think the old girl will make it back to Evans, or shall we try to land it in the treetops? I think we can walk away."

"Rog. It feels and sounds like the blades are coming apart. At this point, we don't know the severity of the damage. You'll have to caress her all the way home. I'm afraid if we pull any extra power, we'll be scattered all over the mountains. Your call, Sir."

That's an understatement! This thing sounds and feels like we're all seconds from death!

"Ok, guys...we're going to attempt to limp back to Evans. I noticed a couple of paddies on the way over here. If we can make it that far, it'll be better than crashing here, rolling down the mountain side, and being fed to the gooks."

"Mayday, Mayday, Mayday! Yellow Five needs an escort. We've hit a stump and have severe damage to our main rotor blades. We're going to try to make it back to Evans. We also have a major casualty on board.

"Rog, Yellow Five. Yellow One will keep you company. We'll be on your tail shortly."

"Thanks for the cover, Yellow One. We owe you."

"We hope you'll never have to return the favor! Yellow One, out."

It's impossible to tell exactly where the blade damage has occurred. Mr. Jewitt is careful not to pull any excess power. The last thing we want to do is shed an entire blade, or even a large portion of one. We're already in deep doo-doo. Calling ahead, the pilot asks for the crash crew to foam the runway at Evans for a running landing that allows for a shallow approach to be made without pulling very much pitch in the blades and adding additional stress to our barely flying machine. The foam allows for a safer landing with less friction, reducing the risk of fire.

Finally getting a couple extra minutes amidst all the action, I unsnap my harness and crawl from my crew chief seat forward to the bloody cabin to assist our wounded. Unfortunately, I'm too late. This man took the machine gun burst through the chest, right upper arm, and neck. Streams of blistering bullets have almost severed his head. His battles are over. I can't help but look into his eyes. Tears stream down my cheeks when I recognize this guy to be... the point man that I met at Evans from 1/9th... Gerry Armstrong.

After what seems like an hour, our twelve-minute flight puts us on final for a shallow approach, and being cleared to land, we see the fire trucks standing by. Jewitt finesses 092 into the long ribbon of foam that appears to be about three feet deep. The aircraft skids to a halt after sliding down the runway for about a hundred yards. Now covered with foam, the aircraft is shut down and the damage surveyed. The last two feet of both blades look like they've been run through a stump grinder! It's a miracle that we didn't crash in the LZ. A helicopter shouldn't fly at all with this kind of damage to its main rotor blades! Now that the flight is finished, we're all badly shaken – almost to the point of having to change our shorts! Typically, during an emergency, even though the tension is extreme, it seems that the full impact doesn't register until it's all over. White Robe Six has protected us once again! Just a few minutes after we exit the disabled aircraft, I have to sit down. My wobbly legs won't support me any longer.

Thank you Jesus!

The field ambulance removes Gerry from the deck of our chopper and takes him to the Evans Grave Registration Station, where he will be processed prior to leaving the country in a flag-draped coffin.

Gerry Armstrong will be escorting his childhood buddy, Kyle Marker, killed two days before. They'll make the Angel Flight together aboard an Air Force C130 that has made hundreds of trips back to the United States. These flight crews have flown this mission hundreds of times; flying America's heroes back to be buried by their families. When they arrive in the States, they'll be transferred to another flight and flown to their hometown.

When the bodies of Kyle and Gerry arrive at the airport near their small rural town, their families and many friends will gather in mourning. Everyone in town knows these American heroes and remembers them as they grew up together riding bicycles, swimming in the local swimmin' hole, playing basketball and baseball, causing a bit of mischief, dating a couple of the cutest girls in town, and saying their final goodbyes to family and friends as they left to fight for their country.

For what did they die?

Walking weak-kneed to the waiting jeep for a ride back to the company area for a well-deserved break, we're all nervous wrecks. We've beaten the Grim Reaper again!

After our break, we walk back to the airstrip to check our ship for further damage. Besides desperately needing a new set of main rotor blades, there are several bullet holes from AK47 and small arms fire. Fortunately, none of the rounds hit anything really important, so we go to work to replace the blades, and put duct tape over the bullet holes. After a couple hours, with the help of the maintenance crew, 092 has a new set of rotor blades that we've tracked and balanced making the ship ready for service once again.

At the end of the day the tally is released at the post-flight briefing. This has been an expensive day for the taxpayers and a frightening and deadly day for a lot of us. The toll is two engine failures with causes unknown, leading to crashes. Four slicks and one gunship have been shot down. In addition, two Chinooks and one Flying Crane crashed while bringing in artillery pieces, ammo, food, and water. We had a total of nineteen comrades killed in action from crashes. Of these nineteen, twelve were crewmembers from several participating companies and the other seven were grunts. A memorial service will follow the post flight briefing. Why do so many young, dedicated men have to die, not only prematurely, but also in such horrific ways? We're all humbled when we realize how fortunate we are to have survived such terrible odds. Our hearts go out to those loved ones back home, who will soon receive the sad news that their husband, father, son, grandson or friend has died in this very unpopular "Police Action".

According to intelligence, there are expected to be at least two NVA divisions in the A Shau Valley. There is not only a good and well-used road down the middle of the valley, but three airstrips that are being utilized by Charlie, and several LZs where they're landing helicopters. Many of the convoy drivers hauling in supplies for the enemy are thought to be Chinese. The enemy's arsenal includes not just the usual automatic weapons and small arms, but they're loaded to the gills with .50 caliber singles and quads, .51 caliber, recoilless rifles, and they have a good accompaniment of 37mm anti-aircraft. They're ready for a long engagement. This valley is not accessible from the east by helicopter much of the year due to weather. But we have a weather window now. We're ready to kick butt, but know there will be many more sad days.

One hundred twelve days to go.

Gilligan's Island. Airstrip and chopper pads right of center.

Two miles SW of Khe Sahn. First time author was wounded.

Tree strike Ashau Valley... Flight back to Evans took about 15.

Waiting out the fog prior to Ashau Valley combat assault.

Bullet hole in Jim Dubose's scout chopper.

Pilot Jim DuBose and crew chief James Owen await rescue after shoot down. Note, they have already removed main rotor blades so their chopper can be sling loaded out.

Another AK47 round through windshield of Jim DuBose's Loach just missing his face.

Rudy Hicks, Gunslinger, Larry Troxel left rear and Medic Burt Beard right rear carrying wounded comrad.

P.O.W.S

Landing Zone

Crew chief Allan Ney with company
mascot Short Shaft.

Crew chief Bill Peterson
between missions.

Letter from sweetheart.

51

CAMP EVANS MAY 21, 1968

Last drink before Ashau attack.

Camp Evans ammo dump explosion
(5 miles away) 6/19/68

Loading up for Khe Sahn.

Village combat asault.

Chinooks sling loading crashed Hueys.

Grunt prepping for Ashau assault.

Loading up C46 Sea Knight.

Larry Troxel, Jim Frost and Kenny Ollie.

Supplies for the field hauled up to log pad by 4WD "Mules" during the monsoons.

Gaggle of Hueys.

Navy, Mekong Delta

Doc Murphy.

WO Ide and WO Jewitt....Great pilots for C/227th AHB, 1st Cav

Chinook re-supply.

Cobra gunship.

North Vietnamese hauling supplies on bicycles

Exhausted grunt ready for another battle.

Americans battling for their lives.

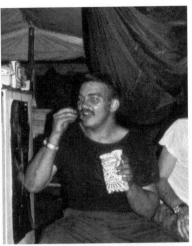

Charlie-Charlie Huey landing at Khe Sahn. Note crashed aircraft that have been pushed off the runway.

Crew chief and great friend, Bob Parent. Shot down and killed in crash on night mission.

Awaiting the next mission outside a Vietnamese village.

Navy River Rats taking a break.

Coastal village east of Hue.

Inserting marines.

Machinist Mate 3rd Ralph Christopher
aboard YRBM 21 Cambodian Border 1970.

Artillery barge in the Mekong Delta.

On patrol.

CHAPTER 8

Stephen ("Shorty") Menendez

Banty Rooster

Tay Ninh 69-70

With the Viet Nam war raging in 1969, the majority of eligible young men wanted nothing to do with it, and tried to avoid it any way they could. However, there were a few who wanted into that mess in the worst way. I guess I wanted to see what war would be like at my tender age of 19, and maybe prove that I could handle myself in battle well enough to stay alive.

I went down to the local Army Recruiter and enlisted to be a grunt. My induction letter came about five weeks later and gave me a date to appear to get my physical. I've never really stood out in a crowd. The reason for that could be because I am only 4'10" and weigh ninety-two pounds. Not much larger than a big Banty Rooster, but very determined. The first clerk who was only a Private, didn't mention my height...he wasn't a Paul Bunyan himself, but after he looked me over, he had a smirk on his face. He just told me to follow the guy in front of me and continue to the next station. This Sergeant began to ask questions with the first being,

"How tall are you, son?"

Well, I puff myself up as much as I can, and in the manliest voice I can force out of my lungs, "Four foot ten, Sergeant". He chuckles softly.

"And your weight, son?"

Wishing I had several large French fries and a couple of milk shakes the night before, I squeaked out,

"Ninety-two pounds, Sergeant."

He can't hold it in any longer. Laughing loud enough to attract the attention of all the other recruits in line, they're all staring at me...and also chuckling. I stand proud.

"Mr. Menendez, I hate to be the one to tell you this, but the minimum army physical requirements are 5' and one hundred pounds. I'm sorry to tell you, but you're disqualified."

"Sergeant, I would like to speak with your supervisor."

While the Major is summoned, I puff myself up some more while trying to figure out what I can say to convince him why I need to be in his Army.

"Mr. Menendez, I understand you have a complaint about being disqualified to enlist due to your stature. What can I do for you?"

"Well, Sir, (now flexing my muscles), I believe I can whip any man here that you put in front of me." (I'm a weight lifter).

With a surprised look on his face,

"Sarge, give me this young man's paperwork. I think maybe we can use him. He has the attitude we're looking for."

With the paperwork signed, little did I know what I was getting myself into.

After going through all the expected ridicule throughout my time in basic training and AIT, I receive my orders for my desired station...Viet Nam.

Twenty-four long hours on the plane and we plunk down on the runway in a foreign country, half way around the globe to fight a dirty, nasty, unpopular war that not one of us understood. As it turns out many years later, no one else understood it either.

Like everyone else that has arrived in Viet Nam, I'm overwhelmed by the blast of heat and humidity that hits me when I exit the aircraft and walk onto the tarmac. Already, I'm having second thoughts about my desire to fight for my country. But hey, I'm here and I can't see any ticket booths where I can buy a return ticket with the seventeen dollars I have in my pocket.

Two days after finishing my "in-processing" paperwork, I receive orders to join my new unit. I'm now a member of C/ 3rd Battalion, 22nd Infantry, and 25th Infantry Division.

When I'm choppered in to my outfit at Firebase Crook, the first thing I notice is that everyone is bigger than me. They all look like giants in their steel pots, flak vests, and filthy, tattered fatigues. Those who are able to shave haven't for what looks like a week or ten days. I notice too, that most of them have turned toward me. It appears they're looking right through me with wide, wild, tired eyes, almost as if they've seen a ghost. Weird.

One of the platoon sergeants introduces himself as Charlie Brown, and helps me carry my gear over to T.O.C. where I meet Captain Schliger. The strapping Captain reviews the Battalion and Company policies with me. This guy is so big, even though he's sitting down and I'm standing, I feel like he's looking down on me. I hate having to puff myself up when I meet bigger guys. Actually, after eighteen years, I guess I'm used to it. It's just a little bit more annoying now that I'm in the military.

Charlie Brown helps me carry my gear to my assigned foxhole on the perimeter where I'll spend the night with two other guys on guard. My new "bunk mates" are Pvt. John Anderson and SP4 Adam Housley.

After the introductions, Adam makes the comment,

"Hey, Sarge, I see we finally got us a Tunnel Rat."

Curious, and new to the business, I ask what a Tunnel Rat is.

"You'll see soon enough. We'll let you know when the time comes."

For a great story of my life in Viet Nam as a Tunnel Rat, see my book: *Into the Darkness*. My second book is entitled: *Battle At Straight Edge Woods*. Both can be ordered on Amazon.com.

Our camp is situated 2.5 miles north of Tay Ninh along Highway 13. It's just two miles from the Cambodian border. Generally, the closer we are to the border, the higher the concentration of NVA. Maybe I'll get some action sooner than I expected.

Spending my first night wrestling with sleep, sweating like I never thought possible with flights of mosquitoes flying formation around me, I'm wondering why I was so insistent on enlisting. I'm quickly learning all about the phrase – "Young and foolish." What an understatement.

Trying to get any kind of rest with outgoing friendly fire erupting periodically throughout the night, while sitting in a nasty foxhole with two complete strangers, and being awakened every three hours to take my shift as a guard, seems to be beyond the call. The final hours leading to dawn end with the welcome smell of coffee. Walking over to the lister bag, I draw some water into my steel pot and take a G.I. bath. Though this is crude, to say the least, it is slightly refreshing. Most of the guys in my new outfit are sucking on a cup of instant coffee or smoking cigarettes. Some are doing both while they break camp and get ready for the next mission. Word has it that the first LZ may be hot.

"Oh Lord, why can't you break me in slowly?"

By 0700 we have our rucksacks packed. Ready to go on my first mission, I'm told it will be an "Eagle Flight Mission". The nature of this assault is for the choppers to pick us up at our current location and drop us into another area to patrol. They'll leave us for two to three hours depending on the circumstances. We'll patrol to another predetermined PZ where we'll be picked up and flown to another LZ with the same mission.

At 0715 our aircraft show up. In a matter of three minutes or so, we're off for my first real adventure with my new comrades. Having never experienced a hot LZ, I'm a bit concerned, so have bummed a couple extra grenades from two of the old timers who didn't think they'd need them. I placed them in the side pouches of my fatigue trousers where I could get at them quickly should the need arise. Though they felt heavy hanging there in my oversize pockets, they did give me a certain feeling of security.

After only a ten-minute flight, our three choppers are on a very short final approach. That's what they call it over here...but I sure don't like the sound of the word, "final".

Just over the treetops now, we've kicked a hornet's nest. Enemy machine gun and small arms fire highlight our approach. I think I hear rounds striking the aircraft, and I'm not at all impressed. I see and hear the crew and my guys getting excited, yelling to each other, rechecking their weapons to be sure they are locked and loaded with one in the chamber, with safeties on. This, of course, makes my adrenaline go through the roof. I didn't know my little body could hold that much. Now I really don't like the sound of "final". The chopper, even though getting shot up, comes to a high hover over a steep hillside. There are real ugly scars of war beneath us. Previous artillery, fighters, and bombers have visited the area and left their deposits. Fallen trees and tall grotesque looking stumps litter our LZ making a landing impossible. The co-pilot turns and yells,

"We can't land, you'll have to jump."

What's he talking about? I'm not airborne!

Our guys are bailing out as fast as they can. They don't want to spend any more time than necessary getting shot at while aboard this Huey. It could be shot down in a split second. Peering over the edge of the chopper deck, I see Mr. Short Guy has drawn the short straw. My only choice of a place to jump is on the downhill side of the Huey and by a quick calculation, I have a free fall of about twelve feet. I'm the last man out and the crew is screaming for me to jump. I'm sure they don't realize that I'm about to puke, but out the door I go. My descent is at Mach .97 taking into account my eighty pound ruck...oh yeah, almost forgot those extra frags in my pants leg pouches. In the split second I'm airborne, the first thing to leave me is my steel pot – keep in mind I did say...STEEL. Even my helmet can't keep up with me. Watching my life pass before me at warp speed, I wonder if the impact will kill me, or if the enemy rounds zipping by will do the job. I figure it will be a head shot since my helmet, that I've been ordered to never be without, is hovering somewhere above me now.

I think I forgot to mention that when my jungle fatigues were issued from the supply room upon entry into this country, they gave me the smallest set they had due to my stature. The Supply Sergeant told me they had never had any "dwarfs" join the army before. Well my waist is much smaller than my pants size and I had meant to tie my britches up with a rope since my belt didn't even fit right. Forgot the rope.

You're probably wondering where I am in my rapid descent by now...way too close to dying.

When my feet hit the ground, I feel the extra weight of my ruck...and those stinkin' grenades. I think my boots only sunk into the jungle floor about two feet. But more importantly, my pants are now down around the tops of my boots! Can't figure out why I was greedy enough to want extra grenades! As I settle in to my landing spot, the enemy is still shooting at us. They haven't hit me yet since they're probably laughing uncontrollably. I'm sure my buddies are doing the same, but at least they're giving me cover fire. In the next nano second, something strikes me like a brick in the head. Yup, my helmet finally came to rest. In the midst of pulling up my pants, I'm waddling off the LZ as fast as my short legs will take me. I think I can hear both sides laughing hysterically over the sound of gunfire. Though this is a most humbling experience, I hope someone has enough sense to be shooting a movie of this once in a lifetime event. At the moment, I don't find it funny, but in forty years, I might be able to look at it and crack a smile.

Fire Support Base Washington is situated along the Bac Si River. Cambodia lies on the other side. Our firebase guards the south end of the Ho Chi Minh trail as it winds its way south towards Tay Ninh. In addition to platoons pulling guard duty on the perimeter every night, each one is on rotation to patrol outside the perimeter each night, to set up an NDP (non-defensive or ambush position) within a half click of the firebase to interdict any enemy that might be approaching the base for an attack.

Two helicopters came to pick our Platoon up about 1000 and flew us out to Hobo Woods where First Platoon was engaged with the NVA. My platoon was acting as a Ready Reaction Force (RRF), and was planning on setting up an ambush. The First Platoon was ambushed on the second day. here, and under heavy contact.

Nearing the sight of the battle, we're flying along at tree top level in an attempt to avoid enemy fire. Looking down from the aircraft I can see a lot of grass huts dispersed between small patches of woods and scattered bomb craters.

When we begin seeing tracers arching through the sky, where our buddies are exchanging gunfire with Charlie, all daydreaming stops. We're very focused on the mission.

Without warning, one of the NVA soldiers is hiding in the brush with a B40 rocket aimed at killing more Americans. The deadly round hits our chopper somewhere in the tail boom. The explosion and horrific shuddering of the aircraft have all occupants of the chopper staring at sudden death, while both pilots wrestle with a snarling out of control monster. The aircraft instantly begins a horizontal spin to the right and starts descending right near the battle zone. The loss of control has been caused by the shrapnel of the rocket damaging the tail rotor drive shaft with the immediate loss of tail rotor and therefore directional control.

Our low altitude puts us in a very poor position to allow for much time to think. The great rotor wing emergency training the pilots received prior to their assignment to Viet Nam helps them to keep their cool, use the emergency procedures they've been taught for loss of tail rotor control, and fly their machine to the ground without killing anyone on board. That's considered a good landing. The bird comes in for a nose low running landing, and the momentum forces the ship's nose into the dry rice paddy. Thinking we're going to flip over, the rice paddy holds the aircraft firmly while the main rotor blades join many other disintegrating parts when they're strewn over a large area. Several of my buddies are thrown clear of the crash while the rest of us escape without injuries. I give a lot of the credit to the great pilots who did their best to keep the helicopter under control. Not to mention "White Robe Six". We've crashed within 100 yards of Second Platoon. Several members of that platoon run from the firefight they're battling to make sure we're all OK, while the rest of their men continue the fight.

We all scramble over to the rice paddy dikes to join in the horrible fight. Enemy fire is pouring out of the wood line and is keeping everyone's head down. We periodically get ammo resupplied by Hueys that do a fast pass and kick it out the doors, but we're out of food after three days. That's the standard load we carry for an Eagle Flight Mission...just three days of food and water. We need those items in a bad way, but the volume of enemy fire is so intense when the choppers come in, they're unable to land.

Several snipers are hidden in the treetops and are giving us fits. Some of our men have been shot by the snipers, and over a seven-day battle, we wind up with twenty-three men WIA.

Two Hueys are shot down in the same area during our operation. The two saddest things in Viet Nam are to see your buddy get wounded, or seeing a chopper shot out of the sky. Whenever I see one go down I feel totally helpless and want desperately to help. I saw it happen too often.

With supporting artillery and gunships, we're finally able to end this horrible battle. The NVA hated when the Americans deployed into firebases, especially when we were located right near the Ho Chi Minh Trail. This definitely cut into their supply program for South Viet Nam.

On the first night we're harassed by mortar fire intermittently. On the second night three enemy brigades (1200-1500 soldiers) have surrounded our remote firebase and at 0215 we're under a full-scale attack. We have three men per foxhole protecting the perimeter. Tomorrow we'll find out that the gooks have cut the wire in several places allowing them to breach our perimeter.

From the berm line, I can see six sappers in the wire. I shoot the first guy, but have to stop shooting when enemy rounds come blazing past my head. The sky is filled with tracers going both ways. I see red tracers zipping out to the enemy and green (enemy) tracers coming from the perimeter aimed at annihilating all of our company. We should have 120 men in our company, but due to combat losses, we're down to eighty-three soldiers. We've set trip flares in the wire in case of attack. They're all burning, as are the hand held flares that we've fired off to help light up the area. As soon as the attack began, we called in for air support. Support is firing beehive rounds (rather than lead, these are filled with steel darts), with the barrels aimed directly at the perimeter. After fifteen minutes of intense battle, Huey cobras and gunships arrive. They can easily see the line between enemy and friendly troops by the tracers and the light of the flares. After hosing the outside of our LZ with mini-gun and rocket fire for just a few short minutes, any enemy that are still alive can't stand the pressure and retreat back into the jungle to lick their wounds. Whenever possible they drag their wounded and dead along behind them.

After this battle, when the smoke clears and we're all trying to recover from the stress and fear that comes with enemy contact, we're all patting each other on the back in congratulations for repelling the enemy once again.

We all had a great deal of respect for the chopper crews. Though we didn't like when they flew us into battle, it was much better than humping. Whenever we were in the jungle and heard choppers nearby, it meant either firepower on the way, they were coming to take us to another place, or they were coming in to pick up wounded or dead. In between those missions, the sound of rotor blades meant ammo, water, food, or letters from home. All were welcome...in that order.

The choppers flew in some awful conditions. It was often rainy with very low ceilings, fog, darkness, or in the midst of a ground attack. Often times it was under more than one of these conditions. The crews were heroes in every way, saving countless lives during the war in Viet Nam. To this day, I look up in admiration when I hear a chopper.

CHAPTER 9

Joe Wasmond

Friendly Fire

There were many occasions during my tour in Viet Nam when we brought overwhelming firepower to bear so quickly, and in such close proximity to our own soldiers in combat, that there was a very real danger of injuring or killing our own soldiers. This could happen at any time, but engagements after dark required extra caution on the part of those delivering this ordinance near our troops.

The hour was after midnight. We were flying another Nighthawk mission over numerous ambush patrols scattered across the rice paddies and jungles. There was no moon that night making it difficult to navigate and figure out exactly where we were, as well as the lay of the land below us. To make matters worse, there were no lighted cities or highways by which we could get our bearings. It was pitch black in the air and on the ground. Pinpointing targets without shooting our own people presented a formidable challenge any night if, and when, we got into a firefight.

We received a radio call from one of the ground units. Their message came in whispered words so as not to be heard by the enemy soldiers approaching their position. This six-man patrol was hunkered down in foxholes near a supply trail as VC soldiers too numerous to engage in battle moved past them.

The enemy was so close to their position they could easily see and hear them. Normally our men would have put strobe lights in their helmets to help me locate their exact position, but this night it was not possible. Nevertheless, they were requesting our gunship support to fire on this trail just a few feet in front of them. I had a general idea of their location simply by the grid coordinates on the map strapped to my leg, but it was very risky.

One of our tactics as pilots was to fly some distance away from these ambush patrols, then drop down to an altitude just above tree top level and come back around. The VC knew we were flying above them from the sound of our rotor blades, but they couldn't see us because we never flew with our lights on. When we were out of earshot, they would think we had flown to another location and were no longer a threat. In reality, we would turn back toward them and drop to the nap of the earth so that our helicopter could not be heard until we were right on top of them.

As I drove the helicopter at maximum speed as close to the tops of the trees as I dared fly, I could see what appeared to be our unit's location. I ordered everyone to lock and load their weapons. Over the intercom I told my gunner to open fire with our mini-gun mounted out the left side of the cargo bay, just behind my seat. The firepower of this weapon was devastating, with the capacity to put a bullet into every square foot of an area the size of a football field. Its use ensured that nothing would be left standing in the target area.

As soon as my gunner pulled the trigger I heard a scream in my headset from the radio operator on the ground. I will take that terrible sound to my grave. He was shouting at the top of his lungs,

"Shut it off! You are shooting your own men!"

Immediately I banked the aircraft hard right and pulled up. This caused my gunner's trajectory to move up along the tree line and tear down some of the jungle foliage. We barely made it over the tops of the trees ourselves.

I thought to myself,

What have I done? Have I just killed some of our own men?

By this time, the enemy knew we were on site, so they scattered into the jungle, dragging with them the bodies of their comrades we had just killed. But I desperately wanted to know if we had just caused some needless casualties of war from our own friendly fire.

When I came back around for a second pass over the LZ, the voice on the radio assured me that our soldiers were unharmed, but that our bullets had come within inches of their foxholes. You can't imagine how relieved I felt that I had not killed some of our own men. Now that it was safer to identify their position and I could see exactly where they were located, I exhausted the remainder of our ammunition around their perimeter and kept watch over them until our fuel supply ran low.

I didn't know the names of the men below us, nor did I ever get to meet them face-to-face. All I knew was their call sign over a radio signal. However, that night, we were all tied together by the reality of the danger and potential damage of friendly fire.

CHAPTER 10

Mike Murphy

Doc

Sept 12, 1968

It is the second week of September and we're out on a routine patrol. We're cautiously working our way through a string of villages in the My Hiep area where we had been previously.

Last time we came through here, we received sniper fire. Today is no exception. Having passed through two thirds of the ville, our point man, Rick Aruda, takes three sniper rounds in the chest. When I hear the dreaded call "Corpsman Up" I rush to Rick's aid. He has just entered a rice paddy from the tree line when he's hit, falling face down in the paddy. Just as I reach my buddy, two NVA soldiers stand up and fire at me with SKS rifles. One round sails into my medical bag, through a couple of compresses, my canteen, and cup, and into my web gear. One round knocks my M16 out of my hands. With no weapon, I grab Aruda's M16 from under the rice paddy water and take both men out.

Now the whole place lights up. We later find out that this is a staging area for a North Vietnamese Regiment. There's a nearby trench that most of us are able to jump into for protection from the enemy fire. Parts of it are booby trapped so shrapnel tears into some of our men.

I bend over and put Rick's body over my back and sort of leap-frog into the trench with him. When some of our men are hit that weren't in the trench, I leave Rick in the trench and run to see who else is hit. Our LT, Paul Ryan, is badly wounded and our machine gun crew has been killed.

The enemy troops are advancing on our now diminished patrol and suddenly they're overrunning us. They're even in the trench bayoneting our men! Our RTO knew we weren't going to make it through this and had already called in a direct hit on our position that would wipe out the enemy...but he also knew in all probability it would kill the rest of us too. But, that would be better than to be killed by the enemy, or taken as prisoners of war.

I hear the first of four Phantoms screaming toward our position. Immediately I lay over the LT and another of our men in the trench for additional protection from the flying shrapnel. The two Air Force fighters drop their 500-pound bombs 'danger close'. The next flight of two Marine Phantoms are almost on top of us; we hear the bamboo slapping the bellies of the aircraft just before they release their napalm canisters right next to our position.

When the enemy fire stops and the smoke begins to clear, I stand up to survey our situation. Upon standing, the rear of my ashen fatigue shirt falls off. I guess it couldn't stand the napalm treatment.

Out of twenty-eight men, we have twenty-two who have been seriously wounded. Our four comrades who have been killed fought heroically with their last breaths, and will go home to never have to face another war. I grieve for them and their loved ones.

Operation Marmaluke Thrust, Phase 7, An Hoa Valley

In the middle of the An Hoa Valley is an infiltration route used by the NVA for resupplying their troops in the south. Winding through the lush valley from Laos, it continues to south of Da Nang. The Tennessee Hill area on the western edge of this valley is always good for a firefight.

It isn't long after our patrol begins that we're again engaged with the enemy. While treating one of our wounded, I'm brutally hit in the side with shrapnel. Our guys call for a medevac. Now, of course, this can't just be a routine medevac where a helicopter comes in and lands in a real LZ. No, we're located on a steep mountainside called Charlie Ridge with tall triple canopy jungle all around and enemy fire – worst-case scenario.

When the H4 chopper arrives overhead, we're advised that the crew will lower a litter basket on a hoist for me to be strapped into. Being a Navy Corpsman, everyone calls me "Doc," not Evil Knievel. I'm not a stunt man and am not at all fond of heights. So my buddies strap me in this birdcage and motion to the crew chief hovering up in the treetops to beam me up. The basket starts its ascent and I'm about to crap my britches when all of a sudden something goes awry and the basket and I start plummeting to earth! After hitting the ground, my "rescue basket" starts its toboggan run down the side of the mountain. Not lookin' too good for the Doc here...until I'm saved by a big rock. After that sudden stop my comrades are quickly at my side, re-hooking me to the cable dangling through the trees. As I'm yelling..."No, no, no..." up I go. Understand, this is all happening during a firefight. I get dragged through a couple of trees on my way to the scariest flight of my life, twisting in the breeze enroute to the closest field hospital. What a wild ride!

Though the memories are humorous now, at the time, I felt a real need to change my undies.

November 1968, Operation Mead River

It's late fall and my company is aboard a chopper for a combat assault on Go Noi Island (Dodge City). When nearing the planned LZ, AK47 rounds and 12.7 mm fire begin ripping into the chopper. Enemy rounds are coming up through the floor and penetrating the aircraft roof. Though this incident catches the attention of everyone on board, it's almost normal until the hydraulics are shot out. Hot hydraulic fluid is spewing all over the cabin and onto the grunts and pilots. Most small helicopters don't require a hydraulic system, because they're easily controlled with normal mechanical linkages. However, when flying the heavier choppers, the aircraft must have hydraulics in order to assist the pilot in maneuvering the chopper. As I understand, most of these heavier aircraft can be flown even if they lose hydraulic pressure. However, it generally takes two pilots on the controls with the "pucker factor" surpassing the red line. Flying finesse is not part of the deal here. The result is often a much less than perfect landing, but often it ends in a severe, fiery crash. When the aircraft is fully loaded, control is even more difficult.

At about 700 feet our bird starts what seems like a controlled spin. We have no idea what's going through the pilots' minds, though they're obviously very busy with the current emergency. The pilots know the outcome is totally in their hands, and the prognosis isn't worth a flying flip. They're able to stop the spin momentarily, before losing it again to another less controlled spin. At 300 feet above the ground, smoke begins filling the cockpit. This is never an encouraging sign. Bullets are still zipping through the aircraft and our eyes are now fully dilated.

When the crew chief yells "Bailout!" from about fifty feet over the trees, everyone has to make their own decision on whether to jump immediately, wait for a lower altitude, or ride out the impending disaster. At a lower altitude, a couple guys make the jump. Miraculously, they land in a muddy river bottom with the South Vietnamese muck slowing their acceleration. The rest of us, hanging on to our "Chariot of Fire" until the last second, are awaiting our death. On the final rotation, the chopper crashes into the trees, scattering helicopter parts all over the jungle. We all survive and are ready to kiss the pilots for a job well done.

After the helicopter parts finish slinging themselves in a 360 degree circle, the radio man comes up to me and claims the back of his head is hurting. Sure enough, blood is running down the back of his neck from a bullet that has entered the spare battery taped to the bottom of his radio, traveled the full length of his PRC25, grazed his head before exiting the top of his helmet, and then through the chopper roof.

Every time our unit landed on an LZ and the rear ramp opened to release it's warriors to the elements, each of us wondered what we would experience this time. I always felt vulnerable wearing my medical bag. I was a prime target for the enemy. After only a few missions, I exchanged my medical bag for a gas mask bag. This effectively masked my identity as a Navy corpsman and I think that was a factor in staying alive while doing my job.

When my first tour was over, I decided to sign up for another with the agreement that I would be re-assigned to my current unit upon my return. Although my wish was granted, I found that the majority of my company had also returned to the States and I found only a few original comrades left in my unit.

During the battle for Hue, I'm the only one in my unit who's trying to save lives rather than take lives. Being the only man in my company during this firefight that isn't wounded, I figured God decided He needed to keep me around to continue patching up my comrades. I'm most grateful for that.

I recall one combat assault when we had several replacements on board. This is their first mission. When the rounds begin to come through the aircraft, it doesn't take any of us long to decide we would rather be somewhere else. When the ramp of the Sea Knight opens we all run out to take our positions in the edge of the jungle; the enemy fire is so fierce several men are hit simultaneously. Sadly, every one of the new men are shot and killed within ten minutes of leaving the aircraft.

CHAPTER 11

Larry Troxel

Gunfighter Six

With three tours in Viet Nam and two Purple Hearts, I've logged a lot of helicopter hours as a Ranger Recon squad leader with the 2nd of 39th 1st Recon, 9th Division Army Rangers. I spent most of my time in the Mekong Delta and the Plain of Reeds.

After having been out for three days, the energy of our company is pretty well sapped when we 're picked up by helicopters and choppered into the Plain of Reeds area near a village that is known as an NVA stronghold. Our aircraft land in a rice paddy about one and a half clicks south of the village and our men unload quickly. Intelligence reports have indicated that a bunker has been spotted in this area by an over-flying chopper the previous day. Our mission is to scout out the village for any current enemy activity. One hundred- fifty yards from the village during our patrol, our point man, Jimmie Bartlett, spots two camouflaged bunkers fifty yards ahead. We notice freshly cut vegetation in the area, so it's assumed Charlie is here. Jimmie falls back to confer with our Company Commander, "Panther Two", LT John Thompson. The "LT" radios "Gunfighter Six", our Battalion Commander, Colonel Schroeder, with a SITREP.

"Gunfighter Six, Panther Two, over."

"Panther Two, Gunfighter Six."

"Roger, Gunfighter. Panther Two is 150 yards south of target with multiple bunkers in sight, over."

Without hesitation, the Colonel chooses to send gunship assistance.

"Rog, Panther Two. We'll scramble the guns to your location ASAP. ETA twenty minutes, over."

Immediately after LT gets off the radio, sporadic gunfire spits out of one of the bunkers. The First Sergeant orders his squads to move and cover to attack the bunkers. In this scenario, one squad at a time moves toward the target while another squad provides cover fire as necessary. We begin a slow, crouching, methodical sneak on the bunkers. After going only a short distance, several more bunkers are spotted, and soon after, we receive additional bursts of AK fire. This wakes up the rest of the unit hiding in the bunkers, and we're quickly fully engaged. Early on, Art Thompson and Dave Jacobs, our fastest and most agile men, attack two of the bunkers and toss grenades in the front shooting ports of the bunkers. This effectively silences those guns. With two bunkers down, we assault more that we hadn't seen previously, utilizing grenades, M16s, M60s and M79 grenade launchers. We soon find ourselves in hand-to-hand combat with the remaining enemy troops. We're getting our butts kicked when, within just a few minutes; we can hear the sweet, sweet sound of Huey blades. Within the next hour, two cobras and a pair of F4s are called in to destroy all the bunkers. Forty-two bunkers are destroyed in the village and surrounding area. 2.75 rockets, 7.62mm mini-gun fire, M60 machine gun, and 20mm cannon fire from the Cobras wreak bloody hell on the entrenched enemy. Napalm canisters and tray-loads of 20mm cannon sparkle from the skies when the fast movers deliver their payloads. The smoke-laden valley is filled with death from above when the stutter of enemy machine guns and small arms fire are silenced at last.

Next to God, the most respected guys were the chopper crews. Without the helicopters, we would have lost a lot more men. Without their support and re-supply, we would not have been effective. If we were in trouble and under attack, and needed ammo or medevac, they would be there to help. There were times when they just couldn't get in due to heavy enemy activity. But, in that case, they would call for more aircraft and usually figure out a way to give us the assistance we needed. There were unfortunate times when they lost aircraft and crews while attempting to do their jobs.

After spending the night during a horrendous downpour just north of the Plain of Reeds area, not one of us got much sleep. Policing up our encampment, we begin our patrol an hour after daybreak. Heading north out of the Plain of Reeds area, the rain comes to a stop and we're moving along quietly on an old trail we find in the now saturated jungle. There are only the sounds of the mosquitoes, monkeys, and birds making their wake up calls. Well concealed in fog as thick as a milkshake Sergeant Ted Swanson, our point man, has set a slow pace while navigating to our target village about three clicks away. In spite of being in Viet Nam, I'm in awe of this peaceful morning that God has created in such a beautiful jungle setting. I'm reminded of a similar day while still-hunting for whitetails with a buddy in Kentucky. We had separated when leaving the truck after our last cup of coffee. Our plan was to encircle a large ridge by each of us walking in a different direction on an old skidding trail. I hadn't been hiking very long when I spotted a coyote jump over a dead fall thirty yards to my left. He disappeared in the swamp before I could get a good look at him, thinking his pelt would have made a nice wall hanging for my den.

A horrendous explosion breaks the jungle silence!

What's left of our patrol hits the deck and we're all hugging the ground. Ted, E3 rifleman from Turlock, California, has tripped a booby trap. The absence of enemy fire tells us the enemy has already left the area and hid the booby trap behind for us to deal with. Medic Paul Johnson quickly surveys the wounds. Both of Ted's legs are missing, blown off at the hips. It's the worst wound I've ever seen; and I gag when I see my fellow comrade lying there in a pool of blood on the jungle floor. I want to look away, but I can't help but stare...perhaps I'm in shock too. I had just spoken with Ted during our water break, not ten minutes prior to the explosion. We were joking about a prank he had pulled in high school. The joke is over. Ted has lost his youthful smile, replaced by a look of horror, after tripping a booby trap. His face is a chalky white, speckled with blood. It appears as if he was caught in a wood chipper and brutally thrown out – without his legs that are now in many pieces strewn about for several yards among the jungle plants. Bone shards from his pelvis are exposed with his mangled flesh. Ted's left arm is badly chewed up to the elbow. Lacerations cover the rest of his body.

Rifleman, Mike Jensen is the second man brutally cut down by the nasty explosion. His right foot is torn off just above the ankle, and it looks like he's lost his right eye. He, too, has been severely sliced from head to toe with shrapnel from the ugly blast.

Baby-faced Bobby Henderson is the third man in the patrol. Though badly wounded with many lacerations, the first two men took the brunt of the explosion.

I have the utmost respect for medics. They're always right on top of the situation and often brave heavy enemy fire when they're called in to horrible situations.

Where is God in this sad set of circumstances?

LT grabs the radio to call for an immediate medevac.

"Gunfighter Six, Panther Two."

"Panther Two, Gunfighter Six, go ahead."

"Roger, we have three men who walked into a booby trap. Request an immediate medevac, over."

"Panther Two, all of our aircraft are currently on a CA. The minute we get one free, we'll let you know, over."

'Roger".

Silence.

While Paul and a couple other guys are frantically tending to the wounds and attempt to stop all the bleeding, the LT removes his helmet. Placing both hands on his head,

"Damn, if we don't get these guys to a field hospital soon..."

The radio breaks squelch and the life-saving sound of helicopter blades can be heard over the vibrating voice of a chopper pilot. As I understand it, helicopters inherently have a one-to-one vibration from the rotor blades being out of balance; and this carries over to the crew's voices.

"Unit requesting Dust Off, Viper Two One, say call sign, location, and SITREP."

"Viper Two One, this is Panther Two. Our coordinates are A6425 and our LZ is currently cold. Over."

"Roger, Panther Two. Viper Two One is about eight minutes out from your location. How can we help you?"

"Panther Two has three men severely wounded who need evacuation ASAP, over."

"Rog, standby to pop smoke when we call a one mile final your location."

"Will do."

"Panther Two, Viper Two One. One mile out. Pop smoke."

The ground guide throws out a smoke grenade to mark their location and the wind direction.

"Viper Two One has yellow smoke."

"That's affirmative Viper Two One, yellow smoke."

As soon as the Huey skids touch down, Ted and Mike are carried in ponchos used as improvised liters by eight comrades. Bobby, though badly lacerated, is able to hobble to the aircraft. Both the crew chief and gunner assist in their gentle loading. Tears are streaming down the cheeks of all eight liter bearers. Not only do they know that their buddies will not return to the battlefield, but they will be missed by their brothers. They can imagine the flood of emotions these warriors will experience when they return to their loved ones.

Upon departure, the rescue chopper turns toward the nearest field hospital to solemnly deliver their passengers. They fly low level over the treetops to save the time they would need to climb to altitude, and to hopefully stay away from enemy fire.

"Viper Two One, Panther Two. As usual, we can't thank you enough for the expedient help. Your crews always come through when we need it most. Super job! "

"Anytime Panther Two. We are always happy to be of any assistance to our buddies on the ground. Have a safe day!"

The airspeed indicator is red lined. After only a couple of minutes, Mike begins to scream and thrash around. He was given a shot of morphine shortly after being hit. He's either in extreme pain, shock, or has just realized the hardships he will face the rest of his life. Ted is lying on the deck of the aircraft, his eyes staring at the ceiling. Blood is speckling his ashen skin every time his heart beats. At least it's still beating. He has no idea what happened, where he is, or his destination. When the extreme shock wears off, he will sadly find out about his horrific condition.

What surprised me on many occasions was when we were in the middle of a firefight, had wounded and dead lying all around, and chopper crews heard our calls for help. Often, they would come in under heavy enemy ground fire. Sometimes, the resistance was so bad the helicopters were unable to land. When able, they would come around for another attempt. Sometimes they had gunship escorts and other times it would be just a slick. They took a lot of hits. Once, I know one of the pilots was hit while on approach. He continued the approach, did the rescue, flew our men to the field hospital, and returned for more. That's the kind of men we could count on daily.

During one fire fight, a Huey came in to rescue five wounded men and was shot down right at our position before we got our wounded on board. One pilot was seriously injured and the rest of the crew came out unscathed. The aircraft soon erupted into a ball of fire. Another bird was called in to pick up the five wounded including the pilot. The enemy celebrates knocking any aircraft out of the sky. That's a huge accomplishment for their side. They love to use them as bait, knowing that another aircraft will be called in to rescue the crew, and yet another to sling-load the damaged chopper out of the area, if there is anything left. In this case, of course, the bird has been reduced to a pile of ashes.

Our company set up a perimeter around the crash site, assuming Charlie would soon surround the area lying in wait for another bird. Within thirty minutes another helicopter from the sister company arrived at the scene. At this time, our LZ was cold having received no enemy fire since the first bird crashed.

"Panther Two, Viper One Niner, flight of 3, SITREP please."

"Viper One Niner, Panther Two. LZ cold at this time. However, use extreme caution. We are assuming more NVA are lying in wait for you."

"Roger, pop smoke and we'll have our two Bulldogs hose down the area outside of the PZ."

"Smoke is out."

"We have red smoke, Panther."

"Affirmative on the red smoke, Viper."

"Bulldog Seven and 'Bulldog One Zero rolling in hot on the east and west sides of PZ."

The gunships are tearing up the turf and hopefully, the enemy that are likely entrenched outside of the PZ.

Small arms and automatic weapons open up on the gunships passing overhead.

"MAYDAY, MAYDAY, MAYDAY...Bulldog One Zero is hit. We're breaking off to the south."

"Roger Bulldog, Bulldog Seven has you in site and will cover you."

The slick is now on short final to pick up the wounded; and the gunner and crew chief are trying to keep the enemy at bay. Tree limbs and roots are careening off in all directions from the heavy machine gun fire. The strong smell of cordite, burning wood, and underbrush mix with the heavy smoke erupting from the jungle and downed chopper.

"Viper One Niner short final. Panther, have your men loaded as..."

"Viper One Niner receiving fire from our left!"

Viper One Niner's voice is heard again with the sound of great urgency.

"Our crew chief has been hit. We're breaking off..."

Another red line flight is in progress over the treetops to the local field hospital. The gunner crawls over to tend to the crew chief's shattered right arm from the elbow to the wrist.

After dropping off the wounded crew chief, Viper One Niner calls Operations to have another crew chief delivered to the hospital pad.

Within just a few minutes another crew chief hops on board and buckles in while the aircraft returns to the scene to try to complete its mission. It's teamwork like this that gets the job done.

Though One Niner took some additional hits on the way in, they successfully picked up their passengers.

You can call this guts or crazy chopper crews if you want to, but I call it extreme heroics! I can tell you one thing for sure. If it weren't for the bravado of the helicopter crews, I wouldn't be here today. I owe my life to those guys. Helicopters are the best things to ever happen to the infantry. They pulled my butt out of some very scary situations! Chopper crews don't get the recognition they deserve.

Our Battalion Commander, Colonel Schroeder, was well liked by our entire unit. He often came out to visit us in the field to see if we needed anything. One day we were in the middle of a big firefight. The Colonel was flying overhead watching and directing the battle when he was suddenly shot down. Unfortunately, he was killed in that crash.

CHAPTER 12

Elmo Johnson

Fish Out Of Water

After basic training, I was trained in the Army Communications School. There I was taught cellular wireless communication off the Mars Satellite. This is what is still widely used today all over the world.

Our entire graduating class went to Viet Nam together and had never had any infantry training. I thought my job would be to fly between secure firebases in a helicopter and set up wireless networks for various military units.

I'm living in a nightmare. I'm totally unprepared for what I'm about to experience.

On my third day in country, a rocket attack begins at 1200 with the first round scoring a direct hit on the mess hall. This is a well-planned attack since the mess hall is full of GIs. When the attack is over, we all rush to assist the injured. Immediately, I realize this is not a nightmare, but a real honest-to-God war. There are 300 soldiers killed and many wounded by the gutless enemy. My assistance is needed to help fill body bags. There isn't a dry eye in the place as we sift through the ruins.

I soon find out that rather than setting up wireless networks, I'm joining up with an infantry unit. The communications between firebases and LZs in the boonies is connected with coax cable.

When communications are shut down, it is generally because Charlie climbs up and cuts the cable. Without radios, the outlying units are unable to call for any kind of support either by helicopters or other air assets if they're too far out in the boonies to use their PRC25's. They're in big trouble. This means that when they're under attack, they're not able to call for ammo, medical evacuation, water, food or additional troops. They can't call for close air support or for artillery fire. They're screwed, the enemy knows it, and takes full advantage of the situation with massive attacks.

When communications are lost, choppers are sent out to search for the cut in the aerial cable. The coordinates are called in, our patrol saddles up, and we bushwhack our way through the jungle to the cut. I'm scared to death! I know absolutely nothing about being a grunt! I'm a fish out of water! When the cut is reached, I climb the pole to repair the cable. Of course, when Charlie cuts the cable, he is well aware that someone will be along soon to repair the problem, so he positions a sniper nearby to wait for me. As soon as I begin the repair, the sniper starts to shoot at me! I'm extremely thin, so learned quickly to get around to the other side of the pole to avoid getting hit. It goes without saying that I also learned to do the repairs in record time! Fortunately, I was never hit.

CHAPTER 13

Allan Ney

They Never Came Back

As a Huey crew chief with C/ 227th Assault Helicopter Battalion, 1st Air Cav from August 1967-68, I have many stories, but the following haunts me even today after all these years.

This story speaks of two of the bravest, unsung heroes of the Viet Nam War. In July of 1968, Eddie Hoklotubbe, a native American Indian from Oklahoma was my assigned door gunner. We were on call on this particular night for any mission that might pop up: flare mission, river sampan patrol, emergency re-supply, or medevac. About 2200 hours, we're called into Flight Operations, along with our two pilots. We're told that an infantry unit is under attack and in desperate need of an ammunition re-supply. This is a tactical emergency.

I only have about two weeks left in Viet Nam. In fact, I'll be released from the Army when I return to the States. Eddie is also very short, after he had previously extended his tour for an additional six months to be a door gunner.

Eddie and I immediately go out to the flight line to place the machine guns and ammo on the aircraft. While we're prepping the ship, our pilots come out, put their gear in the ship, and are about ready to go. Suddenly our Platoon Sergeant, Robert Stone, and crew chief, SP/5 Bob Parent, show up on the flight line and tell my gunner and I to report back to flight operations. The mission has changed.

We head back to the Ops tent to see what's changed and hear our Huey crank up when we're almost at Operations. We watch in amazement, while our chopper lifts off into the very dark night. When we walk into the Operations tent, the Aircraft Commander is relaying a message on the radio for us from Sgt. Stone and Bob Parent. The message is,

"Ney and Eddie are way too short for this mission. We'll see you in the morning."

This crew did not come back from that mission. Whenever a dangerous mission takes place, the crews that aren't flying hang around the Operations tent listening to the radio transmissions to see how their buddies are doing. When these heroes flew into the extremely hot LZ that was under attack, they quickly dumped their load of ammo with the help of several grunts on the ground and took off into a hail of enemy fire. They were shot down and the entire crew was killed.

This was not their mission, but because Eddie and I only had days left in the country, our buddies did not want us to risk our lives. In turn they made the ultimate sacrifice and gave their lives in order to save ours. This happened on a regular basis in this war – soldiers sacrificing their lives, so that their brothers might live.

I knew both men well, but was especially close to Sergeant Stone. For years I have felt extreme guilt over the loss of my buddies. After years of searching, I finally found Sergeant Stone's family. When I visited them, we had a very sad, though good discussion. The family and I are now great friends.

Bob Parent slept in the cot next to me in the crew chief tent. He was always a very jovial guy and we became great buddies. I remember that he chewed mouthfuls of Beechnut tobacco. Whenever he spit, I asked him why he always had to spit it out? I told him if it was that bad, he should quit chewing.

—Bill Peterson

CHAPTER 14

Jim DuBose

Bullseye

When I arrived at Bien Hoa Air Base in 1971 for my second tour, I was assigned to D Troop, 229th Battalion, 3rd Cav.

Within two weeks of arriving, I had passed my in country check ride and was awaiting my first mission. Most of the rest of the unit was out flying when maintenance needed a UH-1 Huey ferried to depot level maintenance. Another new WO-1 aviator and I were tasked to fly the aircraft to Bien Hoa and we would be picked up later.

While en route to Bien Hoa, we were contacted and told to return to Bear Cat and land at the 1st of the 9th to pick up a LRRP team and two door gunners to take them to Brigade Headquarters for briefing.

At Headquarters we were to also get an Aircraft Commander rated pilot from another unit to take command of the aircraft. The two door gunners were from the mess hall and still wearing their mess hall whites, this made them stand out against the olive drab color of the Huey.

When the briefing was over, we still did not have an AC for the aircraft or any maps of the area. However the LRRP team was willing to give it a go if we were, so we took off and headed for their insertion LZ using the maps and directions from the LRRP team leader. Arriving over the LZ at altitude the gun support that was to cover us did not show up so we made the insertion on our own. After clearing the area at tree top level, we climbed to altitude and made sure that the team had radio contact and we headed for Mace Mountain to refuel.

While refueling we were ordered to fly to an artillery fire support base on Highway 1. We informed the TOC that we did not have any maps and they told us not to worry about it. All we had to do was take off, turn left at the highway, and follow it until we came to the firebase.

Arriving at the Arty FSB we joined the three Hueys from our Blue Platoon (Infantry Rifle Platoon of a Cav. Troop), and the Logistic Huey that was flying re-supply missions that day to form a five-ship lift. The Blue platoon infantry had already been inserted into the jungle and was in contact with the VC.

We were inserting an infantry company to support the Blues.

Taking up the trail position in the formation, I called the lead aircraft on the radio.

"Lead, trail's off."

Lead responded: "Roger"

The LZ that we flew into was prepped by artillery and cobra gunships, but as was all too often the case, the LZ was hot and we took ground fire on the way in and on the way out. When we arrived back at the FSB to pick up the next load of troops, the lead aircraft AC called us again.

"Hey Trail, what's your call sign?"

"We don't have one. We've only been here two weeks."

"OK, I guess we'll just call you Trail."

Shortly after this mission I asked to be assigned to the Scout Platoon to fly the OH-6. I loved flying the LOH and was already qualified to fly it. The Loach was normally paired with a Cobra gunship to form what is known as a hunter/killer team or pink team. The term pink team comes from the Guns (red) and Scouts (white). When you combine red and white it produces the color pink.

The missions of the Scouts were to do visual reconnaissance (VR) of an area, to fly convoy support for units moving along the highways, to fly support for units in contact with the enemy, and to clear LZs before the Hueys made their approach and landing.

The crew of the Loach normally consisted of the pilot and crew chief/gunner who was also referred to as the "Torque".

The pilot and the gunner, working as a team, would become very proficient at tracking the VC or NVA through the jungles and rice paddies. It was easy to determine whether we were tracking VC or NVA by the footprints left by their movement. The NVA wore boots; and the VC wore sandals made from old tires that had been thrown away. Judging by the condition of the tracks we could estimate the number of enemy troops, approximately how long it had been since they passed through the area, and whether they were traveling with heavy loads or light loads. This information was critical to the ground troops we were supporting.

Depending on what we found in the AO. Our high bird, a cobra, would call for an artillery strike, hit the target with its own rockets, mini-gun fire or 40mm grenades, or request air strikes from the Air Force or Navy. Since the main rotor blades of the Loach were much quieter than those on a Huey or cobra, we were able to catch the VC/NVA out in the open more often and turn the situation into a good old-fashioned turkey shoot.

The VC and NVA had many methods of moving their supplies from North Viet Nam down to the South. It was not uncommon to follow bicycle tracks through the jungle or mountain passes. The bicycles would be heavily loaded coming south, and leave deep ruts or marks on the trails. The ones going north would barely leave an imprint. The most interesting VC/NVA transportation and warehouse system I found was their use of elephants. On one VR my torque and I spotted what looked similar to loading docks for semi-trucks dug into the ground. The elephants would be backed down the slope and loaded or unloaded just like you would with a semi-truck. When our Blue Platoon was inserted into the area a large bunker complex with connecting tunnels was found next to the loading area.

Of all the different types of terrain that I flew over, I enjoyed flying over the jungle and lower mountains in the middle of the country the most. The scenery was breathtakingly beautiful and teeming with wild life. On many missions we would see spider monkeys, orangutans, wild boars, elephants, and tigers. In the southern part of the II Corp are some of the most beautiful water-falls in the world. The beaches along the coast are spectacular and very inviting. If it weren't for the war, it would have been like spending a year in paradise.

First and last light of the day were exciting missions because that's when the enemy was most active; and we usually got some action. We especially liked river crossings. We would work in three pink teams. While one was scouting, the other two would be wait-ing on the ground at a nearby firebase, each taking their turn when we were low on ammo or fuel.

The last flight of the day, the Loaches would low level down the river and as we passed a village, we'd drop concussion grenades in the water for the villagers. This would bring fish boiling to the sur-face and the villagers would take their canoes and gather the fish for the village. We didn't get shot at from these villages very often.

Some of the grunts wondered why we would basically paint a big bull's eye on the side of our aircraft and fly around low and slow. That was our job. Even though we didn't paint a bull's eye on the ship, Charlie seemed to think we did and we were targeted and hit often.

The LOH was a pretty safe aircraft. It was the smallest helicopter used by the military in Viet Nam, extremely maneuverable and a real joy to fly. The frame around the pilot and passenger area was built like a roll cage. After being shot down a number of times and crashing with neither my gunner nor I getting badly injured, I can attest to the safety of that aircraft.

The most satisfying missions for me were when we could answer the call from a unit that was pinned down. We would fly low and slow nearby to draw the enemy fire away from the grunts, so they were able to get a better vantage point to attack. Helicopters were preferred targets for the VC/NVA, especially if we were low and slow. We were always good magnets. If we could help out our brothers and take the heat off of them, it was all worth it.

91

In the Cav, we were strong believers in no man left behind. There were times when our soldiers were under attack with several men wounded and the LZ extremely hot. If no slicks were available in the area at the time, we would go in and pick up a couple guys. I have even seen cobras go in and have a guy sit backwards on their rocket pod to enable him to be airlifted out.

The enemy was very shrewd. When they cooked their food down in a tunnel, they would let the smoke go out one of the exits with the spider hole being at the base of a tree. That way the smoke would not be easily seen by the grunts on the ground because it would go straight up the tree. Of course we could see it from the air, pinpoint it, and call in the gunships to do their thing.

The LOH had a few areas with very light armor plating, but of course, Plexiglas surrounded us in the front, sides, and top.

My last mission ended when an armor piercing AK-47 bullet came through the bottom of the Plexiglas, went through the left control pedal, and through the inside of my ankle. Another round went into my lower leg. That was the last aircraft that I crashed before being medevaced back to the U.S.

When I was medevaced, my gunner was assigned to another aircraft and pilot. After three weeks of flying together, they were shot down and both he and his pilot were killed. It took two weeks to retrieve their bodies.

CHAPTER 15

Vince Mucci

Spooked

The rule in the Marines for a Navy Corpsman was to be assigned to a company for four months. Two months was spent on a hill in the boonies, and then he was to be transferred to the rear while another Corpsman took his place. It doesn't work that way. I stayed out with my first company for nine months straight. There are usually two Corpsmen per platoon.

The mission of our outfit is to protect Da Nang from rocket fire. We're operating within a fifteen to eighteen mile radius of Da Nang.

While on a patrol in Happy Valley, our assigned mission is to assault Hill 310. The heavy jungle and steep hillside makes our advance toward the top extremely tough. The temperature is around 100 degrees and the humidity is through the roof. To top that off, enemy resistance is heavy and even though we're killing the enemy, several of our men are wounded. The practice of the Marine Corp is to charge up a hill fighting all the way, occupy it for a short time, and then go take another hill. We never set up firebases; we didn't occupy a hill long enough. Often days, weeks, or even months later we would be ordered to go back in and re-take that same hill. Obviously, those of us doing the actual fighting are not making those insane decisions. I can't figure out how the Marines ever came up with such crazy ideas. As a result of poor decisions, we lost an awful lot of American soldiers.

On the first day of my tour, a squad is heading out on patrol. I decide I want to go along, hopefully calm my nerves and get over my initial fear. After humping through the jungle for most of the day, we come upon two crossing trails that are showing recent foot traffic. We decide this is a good place to set up for our night ambush. We set out three claymores per group of four men. We're all set up in a triangular pattern with each group of men connected by ropes for signaling. The plan is to use the ropes for two main reasons. If someone spots the enemy, the ropes are tugged to signal the men in the other positions to be alert. They are also used in case someone falls asleep. Two men in each group will take the first shift while the other two would attempt to get some sleep. The mosquitoes are feasting on me and I don't have enough hands to swat them all. I guess they prefer a new guy's fresh blood.

I'm one of the guys chosen to get some sleep first. *Yeah right! I'm scared to death!* As hard as I try, I don't even want to close my eyes, let alone sleep for two hours. Except for all the sounds of the jungle being new to me, and the sound of the flights of mosquitoes that are on attack missions over my body, all is quiet. I don't remember ever seeing anything as black as the Viet Nam jungle at night. I'm pretty freaked out. Everywhere I look, I see images of gooks sneaking up on us through the darkness. After two hours the other two men tell my partner, Jimmie, and I that it's time for our shift. Oh boy, this should be interesting. At least I know I won't have any problem staying awake. That's my plan for the rest of the night.

After my dilated eyes have been staring into the night for about an hour and a half, someone is tugging on the rope to my left. I tug on the rope to my right to alert the next guys down the line. Suddenly, I hear rustling noises to my left. It sounds like a large animal, possibly a deer, or... is it an enemy soldier sneaking along the trail? Goose bumps fill in the voids where the hair isn't standing up on end. My eyes feel like they're going to pop out of their sockets! Within seconds, I see the first pair of sandals and bare legs pass danger close to my position. They're so close I could reach out and touch them from the bush I'm hiding under. In single file, the North Vietnamese soldiers walk past our position. They're all carrying supplies and weapons. I'm shaking so badly, even the mosquitoes are afraid to land on me. I've never been so scared in my life! When the last of the enemy walks past, an estimated 150 of their soldiers continue down the jungle path.

We call in artillery on the enemy position and, within minutes the NVA that spooked me so badly are history.

For several months, every Corpsman who was out in the boonies was either killed or wounded. I only received minor wounds. Many Corpsmen were wounded severely and were so dedicated they would often stay out in the field of enemy fire crawling to more fellow combatants who were wounded. I don't know how the hell they did it. They're all heroes in my book.

Our patrol is crossing a small bridge one day in the An Hoa area. We're accompanied by a track that's in the lead with several guys on board, when a booby-trapped 2000-pound bomb explodes. The track blows straight up in the air. Running forward to tend the wounded, the track is still smoking and AK47 fire is coming in from all quadrants. I was never known for my fast running ability. Dodging bullets while going as fast as my boots would take me, I headed to assist the wounded about thirty meters away. There's a gook firing an AK who takes special interest in me. Bullets are whizzing all around, but I keep jinxing while running. The AK is a real encourager for me to increase my speed while I run to where the screaming is coming from. When I reach the eighteen year-old rifleman who has been badly wounded in both legs, he's in an extreme panic mode. As soon as he sees me, he asks, "Doc, did I lose them?" Looking at his crotch, I assure him they're still there. That stops his screaming. However, his legs are pretty beat up from several of the gooks stitching him with AK fire.

As a Corpsman, I always carry a .45 that I take out of its holster and lay next to me while working on the wounded. That way, I have quick access to it in case anyone attacks me. My main weapon is an

M14. I like it because it's not only accurate, but fires the same rounds as the M60. I'm a pretty big guy so am tasked with carrying bandoliers of 200 rounds for the M60. The '60 fires the same ammo, so I'm assured of never running low on ammo. I don't care for the M16 as it jams too much. It's pretty susceptible to dirt. In addition, I carry my medical equipment bag, two frag grenades, two laws, flares, and M79 ammo. I also like to carry a shotgun with 00 buck-shot when I can. That's the real ticket for close range work.

One night we get into a real hairy situation after taking a hill. Several hours after dark, we can hear movement all around us. We're surrounded by the enemy. We're a powder keg ready to explode at any minute. The hair stands up on the back of my neck, as I stare intensely into the night. I just know something is about to happen. Will I see another sunrise?

It's creepy quiet on this lonely hill. I begin to shiver...no, I guess I'm shaking...the temperature is around 100 degrees. A blood-curdling scream shatters the stillness! Our wide-open eyes almost pop out of their sockets. We're all looking toward where the scream has come from even though we can't see squat. In a couple of minutes, we learn through radio chatter that PFC Henderson just had an incident with a snake. A poisonous two-step crawled up his sleeve interrupting his already scary shift on guard. The two-step is so named because after it bites you, and you take a couple of steps...you're history. Henderson wasn't bitten, but he sure fright-ened the hell out of everyone. He must have scared all the gooks away, since our perimeter wasn't compromised that night. That snake saved our lives!

The next morning while packing up our gear to move out, a couple of guys spot an antelope way off in the distance. We all have venison on our minds so each of us empties a magazine on it...never touched him...we were too excited I guess. That would have been a welcome switch from c'rats.

After being on hill 502 for two and a half days a Chinook comes in to drop off some food, ammo, and a few replacements for some of our men whose time is up in this smelly jungle. They're headed back to the world. We don't have enough room on this hill for the chopper to land; so the pilots set the rear ramp on the edge of the pinnacle and bring it to a hover while the men are transferred. The aircraft increases power, beginning the takeoff, when it's riveted with small arms and machine gun fire. Settling into the trees on its side, it bursts into flames and rolls down the rugged incline into its final resting place in Happy Valley. There are fifteen members of our company and four crewmembers on the flight. We scramble down to the crash site to assist the crew and our buddies with whom we've spent the last several months living in the jungles of Vietnam, fighting off the North Vietnamese, and saving each others lives. Twenty American bodies have been taken to their fiery grave. There should have only been a total of nineteen men. We never could figure out where the 20th body came from – spooky. Included in the deaths was Milan, a new guy who I've been working with for the past two days. I'm not sure why he was on the flight. He had only been in Viet Nam for a few days. When we were first introduced he couldn't wait to show me photos of his wife and son who had been born just two days prior to Millan shipping to 'Nam.

May 19, 1967 is the worst day of my life. We're patrolling along a path in a box canyon. At the time, I have Curt with me. He's a new eighteen-year old Corpsman that I've taken under my wing, and I'm humping a good portion of his gear. The temperature is right at 130 degrees; and we've all been dragging our butts up a fairly steep slope when Charlie hits us from three sides. We don't know whom we've run into, but while taking cover and returning fire, we soon realize we're in big trouble. The LT calls for air support. Immediately after making the call, he's hit by automatic weapons fire. Gravely wounded, he takes several rounds in both arms. Curt and I rush to his aid. All we can do at this point is stop the bleeding, give the LT a shot of morphine, and treat him for shock while the RTO calls for a medevac.

The firefight continues for another fifteen minutes when a pair of F104s come screaming in loaded with napalm. The lead aircraft dumps his two canisters close to our position. We're all hugging the ground in an attempt to avoid the intense heat and concussion. After lightening his load, the first fighter heads for the clouds while his wingman screams past.

The second fighter comes in even lower. He's a little closer when he pickles his death from the sky. Sometimes when napalm is dropped, the canisters bounce along the ground before exploding. One of these bombs bounces two or three times and then comes apart in a huge explosion. A small piece of the bomb goes airborne and lands on my leg while still burning. It doesn't take me long to fling it off. Though the enemy fire is still coming in, the intensity has been squelched by the life-saving air support of the Navy fighter aircraft. The temperature is at 130 degrees and the humidity is unbearable. We're all exhausted. Without warning, I fall flat on my face. I've passed out from heat exhaustion. A Huey responds to the call for a medevac and the LT and I are flown to the hospital in Da Nang. It's my first opportunity to lie in a real bed since arriving in country. I regain consciousness in the hospital later that day. Tonight we're mortared and I dive under the bed where I stay until the end of the attack. Even though I wasn't conscious, that was my first and only ride in a helicopter during my tour.

After spending the night in the field hospital, I return the next afternoon to the comment, "What are you doing here Vinnie? We thought you were dead?" After laughing that off, I'm told that my buddy Curt took a round in the head and was killed just after I had been airlifted out.

If it weren't for air support, I would have been dead three times over. It was always a gift from heaven. I guess someone was looking out for me.

CHAPTER 16

Larry Troxel

Double Security

Being a "Short Timer" with only sixty-eight days left to serve on my first of three tours, our unit is down for forty-eight hours after some heavy fighting in the Plain of Reeds. We're back at our main Fire Base Barker.

The First Sergeant comes by to suggest that it's time to replace some of the sandbags around our hooch and fire support bunkers on the perimeter. With confidence that our sandbag protection is back in order, we wisely decide to spend some time cleaning our weapons and other equipment.

At 1530 hours all Platoon Sergeants meet at Top's location for a briefing. We're informed by the First Sergeant that things are about to get wild. We're told that Intel Reports that a possible NVA Battalion is planning an attack on our base sometime during the night.

We're ordered to plan on doubling up on all security during the night. In addition the Company Commander has ordered that one of our platoons has to set up an NDP one click out from the firebase.

The First Sergeant looks at me and says;

"Troxy, I know you're short, but the Company Commander has asked that I send your platoon out for this operation. He is briefing your LT now."

Some of the guys in my platoon have only thirty days or so left in country, so I'm not the only Short Timer. I know my men are going to have a hard time swallowing this order, but I also know they have a good history of taking orders.

I call all my men together to make the announcement. As predicted, they aren't all that excited about doing the mission, but did think it would be a wise move to attempt to head off the enemy before they made their planned attack.

We all begin making preparations for the mission. We're not only checking our own equipment, but helping our buddies as well. All missions are important, but for night missions we have to be especially careful. We check to be sure we are not wearing anything shiny and that our equipment is completely silent. We don't want to jingle when we're patrolling or hiding out in the jungle waiting to spring an ambush on the NVA.

I have a couple of guys take their captured AK47s, a trick I had learned from an old timer when I first came into the country. An AK47 has a sound of its own and often tricks the enemy into believing he is firing at his own men.

Leaving the firebase just before dark we arrive at our area of ops, find a great hiding place, and are set up by 2230 hours. Our claymores are set up around our circle of men and we're ready for anything that might take place during the next several hours. We've called in our coordinates to our firebase and to "Puff". They are both on call should we need fire support during the night.

At 0030 hours, our Starlight scope man detects movement about 100 yards out. Now is when our AKs come into play and we open up on whoever is sneaking around out there. If we open up with our M16s or M60s the gooks will know we're Americans.

After just a few rounds returned by them, one of them is shouting and asking who we are and what our unit name is. We have an interpreter with us who shouts back and finds out they're a company of VC. He continues shouting to stall them while we pull up our claymores and begin heading back to base. It's the fastest I've moved at night.

When within about fifty yards of the front gate, the VC realize they've been had and begin firing mortars and AKs at us. We scramble back inside the gate unscathed.

Within thirty minutes, there are VC inside our base perimeter with satchel charges.

We manned the M60 and .50 cal. we had set up outside our hooch to cover our assigned area of crossfire. "Puff" has been called in to strafe the outside of our perimeter and our artillery batteries are emptying their tubes outside our perimeter. The ensuing fire-fight is all over by 0300. At daylight, we all come out of our firing positions to assess the damage.

The enemy has succeeded in blowing up one bunker, two mortar pits, and one security tower. We find four dead VC within our perimeter and after a sweep outside of our concertina wire perimeter; we find thirty-two enemy soldiers who have been killed. Whenever possible, the enemy tries to drag their wounded and dead back into the jungle. The reasoning behind this is an attempt to spoil the moral of the Americans. There are often times after a big firefight that we can't find any dead or wounded, but can see a lot of blood and bloody trails where comrades have been dragged out of sight.

The body of one of the dead "VC" that we find is that of the barber who has been working on base and cutting our hair.

Soon this will all be a memory. Sixty-seven days and counting.

CHAPTER 17

James DuBose

Four Killer Agents

In 1967, 1968, and 1969, I was a Sergeant in the Air Force as an avionics maintenance technician stationed with the 3rd TAC Fighter Wing at Bien Hoa Air Base, South Viet Nam. I worked on the AC-47, Spooky Gun Ship: a terrific fixed wing aircraft that sported three mini-guns on the left side. We also maintained the C123s that were used primarily for spraying defoliation missions. These flights were dubbed "Ranch Hand" missions. We also maintained the radio equipment for three squadrons of F-100s and one squadron of A-37s. We worked on some Army aircraft. If their crews were unable to repair their own radios, we often got the job.

Avionics can be real finicky. Sometimes the problem the pilots had in the air could not be duplicated on the ground, so we would be assigned to accompany an aircraft on a mission to determine the problem. Circumstances permitting, we would repair the malfunction while we were airborne and complete the original mission.

When this problem occurred on one of the Ranch Hand C-123 aircraft, after my task was complete, I would go in the rear of the aircraft, strap into a monkey harness next to the crew chief, and assist him with operating the toggle switches to disperse the 1,000 gallons of defoliant. There were usually two, three, or four birds flying in echelon (formation) making overlapping passes while distributing

102

the Agent Orange, or in some cases, other chemicals such as Agents White, Purple, or Blue were sprayed. The areas of operation to be sprayed determined the chemical we used on each particular mission.

After getting lined up in the formation, the pilot would call "toggles on". When the crew chief and I engaged the pumps, the chemical would go through the spray tubes on the rear of the wings. Due to the prop wash, some of the spray would enter the rear compartment of the aircraft and we would be covered in it. This was not only nasty smelling, highly flammable, and made a mess of our uniforms and the outside of our bodies, but at such young ages, we never really thought about what this may be doing to the inside of our bodies. Thirty-five to forty-five years later, we would find out that lesions on our bodies, breathing issues, cancers, and birth defects are some of the horrendous results of Dow Chemical selling its millions of barrels of poison to our United States Government to be used to help fight an already very unpopular war. A lot of our buddies have died prematurely as a result of exposure to these herbicides.

Agent Orange was sprayed over the jungles of Viet Nam to defoliate single, double, and even triple canopy jungle. Within four hours after it was sprayed, the beautiful green foliage had shriveled up and fallen to the ground. This was a great asset for the U.S. and its Allies fighting in these areas. What was impossible to see from the air through the dense brush was now easily seen: bunker and tunnel complexes, enemy truck and equipment parks, enemy encampments, and supply depots.

The enemy now felt naked, and very vulnerable since we had a birds-eye view of what was on the ground. We were now able to pinpoint these areas and call in the co-ordinates for artillery, fighter, and bomber strikes making it much safer for our men on the ground.

Though these chemicals were very effective in their use, the soldiers on both sides fighting on the ground and those of us in the air were guinea pigs who are now suffering many cancers and life threatening diseases. Birth defects were a cause of Agent Orange as well. Naturally, the civilian population was also affected.

I much preferred doing maintenance at night since it was cooler. One night, while working on a C123 Provider on the flight line, on the west side of the Bien Hoa Airbase, an enemy Sniper took pot shots at me until I was able to get off of the top of the aircraft I was working on. On another night at the end of my duty shift, as I was securing my tool box in the maintenance hanger that we worked out of on the flight line, it came under rocket and mortar attack. An F-100, F-4 and an O-2 PsyOps bird were destroyed. The next morning when I looked at all the shrapnel holes in the wall behind where I was standing I could not believe I was not hit and that I was still alive.

CHAPTER 18

Larry Troxel

Enemy Strongholds

After a day of hopping around from PZs to LZs searching for the VC and humping the rice paddies, we were more than ready to return to our base at Rakeen. We're exhausted and discouraged. We've lost four of our people and have six wounded.

Completing our third search for enemy strongholds, we're waiting for the arrival of the choppers at a PZ. Our platoon is the last out. Our birds are coming in to take us out of the battlefield. Upon landing, Charlie opens up. We all take cover while the six aircraft struggle back into the air. One door gunner is hit; and a second helicopter is shot down just after lift off.

Our platoon immediately takes cover and after being sure the crew has escaped without serious injury, we fight off an enemy onslaught.

After a two-hour battle we call in for air support, and within fifteen minutes, two cobras are overhead spraying mini-gun fire just outside of our flanks. In just a few minutes, the gunships clean up the mess.

Gunslinger, our CO, calls down from his Charlie-Charlie aircraft. During most operations, the CO flies overhead at around 1500 feet. This is a pretty safe altitude to keep a chopper out of the reach of automatic and small arms fire. He helps give direction and call a lot of the shots for his unit below. As RTO, I receive the call and give the hand set to LT.

Bad news. We're ordered to insert our platoon at coordinates A213426 to search for possible NVA troops in the village.

At 1630, we're inserted one and a half clicks from the village. There are paddy dikes and a wood line on either side of the village. Exiting the aircraft, my gut is churning. The only good thing I can see is that we have a cobra hanging around.

Advancing within one half click of the target area, suddenly we're the target! We're receiving enemy fire on both of our flanks. Maneuvering forward under fire, we soon find that this is a bad move. We're squeezed into the hard-core NVA to our front. They're like a swarm of hornets on a blistering hot day. Air support is immediately called in to wreak havoc on the enemy. Our friendly cobra pilots light the place up. A Wart Hog is also nearby and joins in on the battle. What a pretty site! They make quick work out of either killing the enemy or running them off to lick their wounds. This was a very short battle, with one wounded helicopter gunner and thirty-five enemy killed. Thank God for good communication and air support!

After returning to Rakeen, a cold shower, hot meal, and most of all, twelve hours of sleep are most welcome.

Early the following morning we're inserted for another search and destroy mission. While patrolling toward a village LT, an OCS graduate, gives the order to search a bunker and hootch just ahead of us. I see signs of booby traps ahead and have just begun to tell LT when he stepped through the door of the hootch. There's a tremendous explosion! Doc Bare runs forward and finds that the LT will be returning home. One leg is severely mangled and the other is missing. Another close friend is wasted by the enemy. There is no end to this madness! Who will be next? To a man, we're all understandably paranoid.

When I notify Gunslinger on the PRC25 of the tragedy, he immediately calls for a dust off and finds that their aircraft are at least thirty minutes away. Realizing one of his men could easily die from blood loss or shock; he gives me a shout on the radio,

"Alpha 31, pop smoke, we'll land immediately to evacuate the wounded."

"Roger Gunslinger. Smoke is out."

"Confirm yellow smoke. Over."

"Roger. Yellow smoke."

Landing in front of our ground guide, the CC chopper lands amidst the swirling smoke to take one more precious soldier out of the bush. This is one Battalion Commander that really cares for the men under his command.

CHAPTER 19

Ralph Christopher

Dung Island

Duty Honor Sacrifice may be purchased from www.Authorhouse.com, Amazon.com or book stores in America.

Enemy contact continued at a steady pace throughout the year, with Brown Water Naval Forces heavily involved. Time and time again, Seawolf gunships scrambled to support and rescue friendly forces, putting themselves into harm's way. VC insurgents aggressively transported resupply munitions and weapons from the Ho Chi Minh Trail into Vinh Long Province via the Mekong River trails. Routine procedures found the Viet Cong reinforcing crossing points with extra fighters to ensure safe passage along their routes deeper into the delta. One of these Viet Cong trails was Dung Island, which was a major Underground Railroad waypoint for VC logistics and operations. Located near the mouth of the Bassac, midway in the stream, Dung Island provided refuge, shelter, and desirable cover for enemy elements transiting the landmasses of the coastal plain of the Long Toan Secret Zone on the north side of the Bassac. It was said to be a stop-off spot for the Viet Cong traveling between Saigon and the U Minh Forest with arms. It was a hot area that claimed the lives of many good sailors.

Less than a year earlier, on July 11th, 1967, Boatswain's Mate First

W.V. Potter, Gunner's Mate Third O.P. Damrow, Seaman R.L. Center and Fireman D.R. Nelson were lost when the enemy detonated a Claymore mine directed at their PBR near the northern tip of Dung Island. This happened when six river patrol boats of River Section 511 were in column returning to USS Garrett County, LST 786, on the Bassac. Moments after the mine showered PBR 58 with shrapnel, patrolmen on the other PBRs saw six Viet Cong fleeing the area and took them under fire, killing at least three. Seawolves launched and struck the enemy sites in the tree line.

The following recollection was provided by Seawolf Pilot Lieutenant Matt Gache, who flew Seawolf One-one off the USS Garrett County.

Our fire team had the duty that day. Lieutenant Tom Greenlee was the fire team leader in the lead gunship, with Lieutenant Webb Wright as his co-pilot. I was his wingman in the second bird, with Lieutenant Junior Grade Mike Jaccard as my co-pilot. Tommy Oleseski was my regular door gunner sitting behind me, and Chris Maher had the left door gunner position. We were out on the flight deck, enjoying the warm sun, observing a PBR patrol returning to the Garrett County. We were anchored up river from Dung Island on the Bassac. The PBR patrol was coming up river on the south side of the island when we observed one of the boats moving over to the shore. All of a sudden, we saw a burst coming from the tree line, most likely a Claymore set up in the trees. It hit straight on, and the boat went dead in the water. We scrambled to the island and put a strike into the tree line. I don't know for sure if we did any damage. In the meantime, the cover boat had gotten over to the PBR that had been hit and towed it back to the ship. At the time, we thought there were several wounded on the boat, so we were called back to the ship to medevac the wounded to Soc Trang, the nearest medical facility. Tom's crew took two wounded aboard their chopper and my crew took two, but when I looked in back of the bird, both of the PBR sailors looked pretty bad. Unfortunately, none survived. It was determined later that they had taken their helmets off, since their patrol was over and the home ship was in sight. I remember that the PBR river section officer in charge was furious with the survivors because they had thrown caution to the winds. The men that we medevaced had severe head wounds and might have survived had they been wearing their helmets.

Two days later, Seawolf One Seven was shot down at Dung Island and landed hard into a muddy rice paddy killing crew chief, Aviation Machinist's Mate Third Donald F. Fee, and injuring the other three crew members of the downed chopper. Navy Pilot Lieutenant Commander Jimmy Glover did the best he could, but it was a beat-up old bird that, after she was hit, froze up and came down fast.

Petty Officer Fee, a West Virginia native who had just extended his tour and was one of the original Seawolves of Helicopter Support Combat Squadron One, had his gunner's safety belt fully extended so he could lean well outside the aircraft and engage enemy troops from all possible angles, including underneath the bird. When the gunship smashed into the rice paddy, the copter's rolling momentum propelled crew chief Fee out to the full length of his restraint outside the cabin of the copter. As the fuselage rolled over, Fee became trapped outside the cabin door and was ultimately buried under the bird as it rolled onto its final resting position in the mud. As the crew was extracted from the wreck, Pilot Jimmy Glover saw an arm waving from beneath the fuselage. It was Fee, trapped in the thick mud. The crew tried to lift the copter up while Glover attempted to pull Fee free, but it was impossible. Glover held Fee's hand tight as Fee squeezed as if to say, "I'm trapped; please help me." Glover squeezed back to say, "Hang on, we are with you and trying to dig you out," but there was just no way. Crew Chief Fee drowned in the sucking mud of Dung Island.

Losing Fee hit all of us hard, especially Jimmy. Our Seawolf Detachment Three leader, Lieutenant Commander Allen Weseleskey, had been replaced by a train wreck that had been trained by an-

other detachment and would not take our advice on anything. He took his wingman back to the target area three times approaching from the same direction. Jimmy Glover advised the flight leader to not go back in from the same direction. You just didn't do that. The lead ship wakes everyone up, and the wingman takes the hits. Well, it only took one round that hit the fuel line and the engine flamed out. Jimmy was flying low over the rice paddy at an altitude where recovering from a flameout is virtually impossible. In the rotor head world, it's called the dead man's curve.

—Matt Gache

The second helicopter in the fire team rescued the surviving crew-members and took them to Soc Trang for treatment. Fixed-wing aircraft struck the enemy positions and a landing party from Vietnamese Coastal Group Thirty-Six, escorted by six PBRs, was dispatched to the scene. The landing party met light opposition in reaching the wreckage that had already been partially stripped of weapons, ammunition, and documents by the Viet Cong. A search of the area by the Vietnamese sailors uncovered the missing items hidden in a hut. After the body of Petty Officer Fee had been recovered from beneath the stricken helicopter, it was extracted by a heavy-lift helicopter. The landing party withdrew under covering fire provided by the PBRs and Seawolves.

Shortly after Seawolf One Seven had gone down, PBRs had requested permission to go in and recover the crew of the downed bird, but were denied permission. The PBR crews had decided after this tragic event to never request permission again, and agreed in the future to go in to assist any and all Seawolf gunships, on whom they relied heavily during combat actions. The PBR crews were saddened by the fact they were not allowed to go in to help their Seawolf brothers and this would affect future decisions.

Battles raged on around the island for the next year with light casualties. Then on July 13th, 1968, while on a routine surveillance patrol, Seawolves One Three and One Seven, which had been overhauled and drafted back in service, received permission to place a strike in the northeastern section of Dung Island. The two gunships dove in receiving fire from all quadrants. Seawolf One Seven announced "going down" and was observed in a right descending turn with rotor RPMs decaying extremely fast. The chopper came to rest in heavy underbrush after crashing. Seawolf One Three broadcast "Mayday," and rescue aircraft were scrambled. SEALs who had been operating on the western bank of the Bassac across from May Island were told to abort their mission and return to USS Harnett County for transportation to the crash site. In the meantime, the wreckage was located by Coastal Group Thirty-Six personnel, who guarded it along with Popular Forces from Long Duc Outpost until the next morning, when PBRs inserted the SEALs for the completion of the salvage work. All four crewmembers, Lieutenant John L. Abrams, Lieutenant Junior Grade James H. Romanski, Aviation Metalsmith Third Raymond D. Robinson, and Aviation Metalsmith Third Dennis M. Wobbe, were lost in the crash. After removing as much of Seawolf One Seven as could be salvaged, the remainder of the copter was destroyed by C-4 explosives by the SEAL Team.

The SEALs continued to conduct special operations on Dung Island and in the Viet Cong Secret Zones along the coast. Binh Dai, Thanh Phu, and the Long Toan Secret Zones were all well known Viet Cong hideouts. The U.S. Navy and Coast Guard units fought the Viet Cong for control of these inlets to the Bassac and Mekong Rivers from the South China Sea, but the VC stubbornly refused to give them up.

CHAPTER 20

Joe Wasmond

I Will Never Forget

I had always wanted to see the Vietnam Veterans Memorial or "The Wall" as it is now referred to. In order to construct it, a 500-foot slice was taken out of the ground in the middle of the park. The memorial consists of two walls with the East Wall pointing to the Washington Monument and the West Wall pointing toward the Lincoln Memorial.

The material chosen for the memorial was black granite. The chiseled names of every soldier who died in Viet Nam in that granite rock monument turns white so you can easily see the 58,267 names of those who lost their lives in Viet Nam to stand out boldly. Two hundred forty-four of those soldiers were awarded the Medal of Honor. One hundred fifty-three of them are on the Wall. The granite is so highly polished that it acts as an almost perfect mirror. As you stand in front of it in the sunshine, you see your image reflected back. It is a stark reminder that, though the names of the dead are engraved on the wall, we on this side of life cannot reach them and they cannot reach us.

If you have never been there, it is not easy to find even in daylight. We approached from the north side and didn't see it until we were on top of it. I started down the walkway in front of the wall. I soon noticed the flowers, pictures, cards, and personal items left in front of the various panels by relatives and friends that mourned the loss of a family member who died in this war.

As I reached the dividing point between the east and west walls, I stepped back onto the grassy knoll behind me and sat down. The Wall was lit with lights. It was raining and cold. Gazing at the memorial, my emotions hit me like a runaway truck. I was overwhelmed and began to weep uncontrollably.

Both Kathy and Sarah came over and just held me. The young woman who waited until I came home from the war to marry me, and my youngest daughter, Sarah, who was born to us ten years later was now comforting their husband and father. Neither of them said a word. But they understood that a soldier had come home, and my girls were there as I wept.

After a few moments, Kathy and Sarah left me alone to look for the names of my fallen friends inscribed on that black granite wall, like Sugi and others to help me remember my fallen comrades. They give us these pieces of paper to place over a name to etch that name onto the memorial paper with a pencil.

It was a trip I shall never forget.

CHAPTER 21

Larry Troxel

Bursts Of Mini-Gun Fire

On June 3, 1968, our unit is en route to conduct a sweep at the Plain of Reeds in the Mekong Delta. On our helicopter approach to the LZ, we start receiving fire from both sides. Our chopper gunners are returning fire and are joined in unison by two gunships on either side of the flight. Man, can those guys lay down the lead! The bursts of mini-gun fire is ear shattering, but sounds so smooth that it's hard to believe that it's a gun firing so rapidly. The pilots can't fire continuously or the six barrels of the gun will get so hot they will be inoperable if not allowed to cool between bursts. Accompanied by rocket and 20mm cannon fire from the gunships, I wonder how the enemy can possibly survive the onslaught. Though many are killed, we soon find out that all the enemy hasn't been put out of action.

Exiting the slick, our last two men notice that one of the gunners has been hit. Sgt. Shindledecker and SP4 Blessing rush back to check on him, even though the LZ and chopper are under heavy fire, while the rest of the platoon lies down cover fire. They find the young man has been stitched across the shoulders with AK fire. Unfortunately his Purple Heart and other medals will be awarded posthumously like so many other guys in this "Police Action".

The chopper had entered the LZ with our men and a crew of four. It departed under daunting fire with a crew of three and one crewmember KIA. Why can't this madness stop?

After about a fifteen-minute firefight in the LZ, the enemy fire stops. Either we've killed the little suckers, or they fled. Either way, we can continue our mission.

Our second platoon begins a sweep south of the tree line and canal, while first platoon sweeps the north side. A Scout chopper is up ahead and the crew appears to have spotted something, but at this time, we can't see what it is. The crew chief drops a CS canister on the camouflaged enemy. The chopper was upwind from our platoon so we got a good whiff of gas up our nostrils and in our eyes. We don't carry gas masks, so we continue while trying to see with our stinging eyes. The pilot drops his bird down over the canal where the rotor wash is blowing branches back along the bank, revealing two VC hiding in the water, waiting to ambush us. They're quickly dispatched with machine gun fire from the "Little Bird".

Had we continued our mission without the Scout team, we would have walked right into a nasty surprise ambush. It's anyone's guess how many of us would have died.

As always, the sound of choppers coming in to our area meant some kind of relief. Either they were coming in to pick us all up following a mission, bringing ammo, food and water, to fly protective cover while we're under attack, or quickly and heroically flying in to rescue our battle torn wounded. When the enemy activity is slowed or halted, these crews land to escort our dead. Body bags are loaded on board, for their final chopper flight to Graves Registration. When this type of mission is in progress, our mantel of bravery and heroism is replaced. We're a bunch of teary-eyed boys who left high school, family, and sweethearts to fight for America's freedom. Is it all worth it?

CHAPTER 22

Sarah Wasmond

Horrors That No Human Can Fathom

"Sarah's recollections of that night are poignant and pro-
foundly meaningful to me. She wrote this in her journal while
she was still in Junior High that night after the trip and gave it
to me years later to include in my book entitled, *Battle Plan
For Spiritual Warriors.*"

—*Joe Wasmond*

The dark shadow of The Wall swallowed my sight as I searched for
my father's silhouette. The myriad of engraved names moaned with
memories of the soldiers' souls. They told of terror and triumph,
death and duty, suffering and salvation. Drizzles of the rendering
rain dampened my pencil and paper until I reached the place on
The Wall where my father found the names of his friends. Each engraved letter loaded my awareness of the missing link to this father
of mine. Trembling, my dad turned to hold me, but to my astonish-
ment it was not him. Facing me was a nineteen-year-old boy who
had seen horrors that no human can fathom. Tears that I had never
seen him shed before poured down, dropping him to his knees. So
overwhelming was his grief, that I didn't know what to do or say to

117

comfort him. So I proceeded to trace the name of the man that burned to death before my helpless father's eyes. While each letter lifted onto the paper, the understanding dripped into my conscious mind. The reflection of the names rippled, revealing the reason for rejoicing as I realized I was not replicating my father's name. I looked in awe at this man who attempted to provide and protect what he felt was true. I understood what he had lost in order to have fought. I had seen him as a carpenter, missionary, pastor, leader, speaker, and teacher. Now I could say I knew him not only as a spiritual soldier, but as a veteran of a war that I would never understand. I am so proud to have a father and friend who has survived and surpassed the Viet Nam War. That was his boot camp for the spiritual war he now fights daily. I praise the Lord who gave me my father and who promises us victory in this life and immortality in the one to come. Thank you, Dad. I had a hard time finding the right words to express myself. I am sure you had it a million times harder. I am so glad you are alive and strong, inside and out. I love you so much and am proud to be your daughter.

—Your Daughter,
Sarah

Bibliography
Wasmond, J. *Battle Plan For Spiritual Warriors.*

CHAPTER 23

William E. Peterson

The Last Mayday

Specialist 4 Paul J. Hansen is a good friend from Idaho who is one of our gunners. He lives with his parents on a horse ranch several miles outside of Bozeman.

Paul has only one week left before he will be leaving the field to be processed for his long awaited return back to the world. He was a member of our unit about three months before I showed up. When I arrived in country, he and I hit it off immediately. We both live to hunt, fish, and trap. We've made plans to get together in Idaho for an archery elk hunt. In exchange, he wants to travel to my home in Michigan to fish salmon on the river that runs right past the door of my mom and dad's cabin.

The countdown on the calendar he has printed on his helmet shows he has only a few days before his tour will end. He doesn't have to fly any more missions, but he says he wants to go on just one more flight before leaving for home. Even though it will put him in danger again, like all of us, he likes the adrenaline rush. This particular combat assault is expected to be a very hot one.

Several of us try talking him into staying on the ground, but his mind is made up. He volunteers to fly the mission for the assigned crew.

Tim is the gunner on the "Charlie-Charlie" aircraft that's flying over the battle zone. Their job is to oversee the firefight, and listen in on a large bank of extra radios that have been loaded onto the aircraft. Generally, this is a pretty safe flight. We have only lost one CC in the last several months.

Having an overhead view can be very advantageous to the grunts on the ground. If enemy troops are spotted, the Company Commander on the ground can be forewarned. If the Aerial Commander can see changes that might be made to enable the American troops to have more advantage, they're quickly discussed over the radio.

In addition to the two pilots, are the Crew Chief, Paul, a Colonel, one Major, and a Master Sergeant. These passengers are the eyes and ears for the battle raging below.

Flying at 1500 feet the aircraft is fairly safe from small arms fire, even though an occasional tracer is seen whizzing in their direction.

Our crew is assigned the Yellow Three slot in the flight of choppers. We'll be the third aircraft into the LZ. When a hot LZ is encountered, sometimes the first bird in is hit and crashes in the LZ. There have been many times that the enemy waits for several ships to land before they decide to open up. This is always a crapshoot. My ship is the most powerful in the company according to most pilots who have flown it, so the Flight Leader can choose his aircraft and, therefore, the crew chief he wants. Often my aircraft is the bird of choice for flying "Yellow One". I have never felt lucky or unlucky to crew the first bird in the assault. There are times when it doesn't make any difference. Often, all of our aircraft are shot up.

As soon as the first ship, Yellow One begins their approach into the LZ, the jungle below erupts into a frenzy of automatic weapons fire. Our flight escort of cobras lights up the enemy below with rockets and mini-gun fire.

Our flight of six slicks carrying the grunts is in a fairly tight trail formation. As soon as Yellow One unloads its troops, Yellow Two makes a rapid approach with a deep flare ten feet off the ground to slow the aircraft and comes to a quick hover about five feet off the ground when the seven grunts bail out, and scramble for cover.

Both Yellow One and Two have taken several hits. We take a few hits on our approach and the cobras are still doing their thing. We join in with our machine guns until our barrels are hot.

Glancing down into my box of belted 7.62 ammo; I realize I've expended almost half of it. After departure and enroute to pick up more infantrymen for another lift, I'll have a few minutes to reload my ammo box from the other boxes of ammo that I have stored under my seat. One of my big nightmares is running out of ammo in the middle of a firefight.

The jungle foliage is being savagely ripped apart from all the gunfire. Trees are falling in the LZ from being struck by rocket fire. The grunts who are already on the ground are laying down cover fire with their M16s and M60 machine guns in an attempt to help keep the enemy's heads down and hopefully protect the incoming helicopters. The entire LZ is filled with smoke. The smell of cordite, jet fuel, hydraulic oil, sweat, and burning jungle combine to produce a smell like none other.

On our approach we experience the same heavy enemy fire and can hear the bullets pinging on both sides of the aircraft. Now we have to be very careful to only fire on the outskirts of the LZ to keep from killing our own men.

As soon as our chopper reaches about a six-foot hover our warriors exit the aircraft quickly. I feel sorry for our guys every time they have to jump out. They have sixty to eighty pound packs on their backs and occasionally twist or break ankles or legs. When this happens, they are laying on the LZ under fire when the medic has to rush in to drag them to safety for stabilization. During that time, other men are often hit and need the attention of the medic too. However, the majority of grunts feel very vulnerable in a chopper. Most of them have seen choppers shot down so they want to get on the ground and find cover as quickly as they can.

We take a few more hits departing the LZ. The pilot makes a tight turn and reaches for the sky in an attempt to evade the enemy. While the Aircraft Commander is flying, the co-pilot always keeps his hands close to the flight controls, just in case the pilot is hit and taken out of action. It takes but a second for the aircraft to go out of control without someone on the controls.

121

We can hear the CC Commander giving orders and see him circling above. Gaining altitude and flying toward the CC aircraft, we see a small fireball when .50 cal. rounds strike their aircraft.

"Mayday, Mayday, Mayday. Bull Dog Six is hit. We're going down."

"Bull Dog Six, Yellow Three has you in sight. You're on fire! Get on the ground...FAST!"

Performing a very rapid auto rotation, the CC aircraft heads for a nearby rice paddy. At this point, they are all assuming they will safely auto rotate and our ship will rescue them. However, they also realize that they will land amongst the enemy. The gunners are laying down machine gun fire into the area surrounding the proposed landing site.

Receiving fire on the way down, the pilots are pretty frazzled. All helicopter pilots are fully aware that an auto rotation has to be perfectly executed in order to have a safe outcome. With the ship on fire, the crew and passengers want desperately to get on the ground. With the aircraft descending far too rapidly, the pilot attempts to recover but the aircraft makes an extremely hard landing. The ship lurches forward in the stinking muck. With the sudden stop, the main rotor blade disc tips rearward and cuts the tailboom in half. The ship rolls slightly to the right and the main rotor mast twists and tips over onto Paul's back, effectively pinning him against his machine gun mount.

Parts of the Huey are scattered all over the wet, smelly rice paddy. The bird has come to rest in a fiery grave with the aircraft magnesium now burning ferociously.

Within thirty seconds, we land as close as possible, but far enough away for protection if the disabled aircraft explodes.

My gunner, Eddie Hoklotubbe, and I race through the muck with our ship's fire extinguisher. We're still receiving small arms fire from a nearby tree line. The heat from the burning magnesium is hotter than hell itself and no match for our small extinguisher.

We're only able to get to the Colonel in the cargo bay. After releasing his seat belt, Eddie and I grab him by the arms to pull his lifeless body from the wreckage. Eddie has the Colonel's right arm that is already badly burned. I have his left. The skin on his forearm slides off in Eddie's flight glove – a very gruesome sight.

There is no sign of movement. It appears that everyone has been killed. My gunner and I can't stand the heat anymore. Running from the heat and expecting an explosion at any time, one last look back and we see Paul still moving even though he is pinned between the mast and his machine gun.

We have to save our buddy! Attempting to free him from the weight of the heavy rotor mast, we find that even though our adrenaline is going through the roof, we're unable to budge it. We have to retreat from the incredible heat again. Looking back, Paul's clothing is now engulfed in flames.

Watching from several yards away in anguish; helpless we both have tears mixing with the sweat on our faces. Though writhing in pain, Paul is looking at us with saddened eyes. Still they seem to have a look of appreciation for our failed attempt to save his life and the lives of the others on his ship. His haunting gaze also has a peaceful look even though he is within seconds of death. I know he is a believer, and he is going to a much better place.

The smell of burning hair and flesh mixed with that of the burning aircraft, hydraulic fluid, fuel, and oil are unforgettable.

When I think of this crash, even today after forty-five years...I can still smell that distinct smell of my friends being cremated right before my eyes. There are no screams of horror from Paul or from the dead. Only the sounds of the war bird burning into oblivion.

The families of each of these warriors are anxiously awaiting the return of their hero.

All of these valiant men died when their chopper was shot out from under them. I was good friends with all of the crew and had previously flown with both pilots.

Paul's loved ones are back in Montana anxiously awaiting the return of their soldier. They're planning a big family gathering for his homecoming where the table will be loaded with his favorite foods. His girlfriend of three years has been invited, of course. She has spent the last twelve months writing to and dreaming of her lover. She's anxiously awaiting Paul's return and can hardly wait to be swept up in his muscular arms. We often talked about our sweethearts and, of course, couldn't wait to get back to them.

Paul's brother, Bobby graduated from high school three months ago and has signed up to go in the Army. He's scheduled to be inducted next week hoping to be a hero like his brother.

Bobby has the hood up on his car in his parent's driveway where he is working on an oil change. Hearing another car pull behind his, he looks to see two men get out of an OD government car. Instinctively, he knows this is not going to be good news.

Awkwardly greeting the Major who is a Chaplain and the Specialist Five, decked out in their Class A Army uniforms and wearing highly polished shoes, he leads them to the front door and asks them in. His mother is in the kitchen baking and his father is tinkering in the basement. Today is Saturday so everyone is home. Bobby decides to go down to tell his father about the two military men in the living room who want to talk to him and his mother. When Bobby and his dad walk into the kitchen, his teary-eyed father walks over to his wife of twenty years and gives her a hug.

"Honey, we have visitors."

Rarely has she seen her husband in tears. At this moment he has good reason to be crying. Turning white with fear of the unknown, while walking slowly into the living room, her tears come quickly. Greeting the two soldiers, they know they are facing what they have feared the most ever since Paul left to serve his country.

Following the brief introductions, the Chaplain shares the condolences of the United States of America and the U.S. Army. After he explains briefly that their son, Specialist 4 Paul J. Hansen, has been killed in the line of duty while in Viet Nam, the Major explains that they will be notified as soon as the date of arrival of their son's remains is known. It may take up to two weeks.

A contact number is left and the shocked mother, father, and brother are assured that the military will keep them informed. While the two gentlemen walk down the front porch steps the door closes.

The tear ducts open wide on all three family members while they ask God – Why?

Shocked into the reality that their son has died at the hands of the enemy while fighting for freedom, is a parent's worst nightmare.

After an hour or so, Mr. Hansen begins to make the dreaded phone calls that he had hoped to never have to make. He called family members first and then other loved ones to tell them of their tragic loss. He then called all of Paul's friends to break the sad news.

The next morning, necessary plans to bury their nineteen year old begins. The Chaplain told them that an open casket for viewing would not be possible. Just three days ago, Paul was one of the heroes that burned to death in the helicopter crash.

There will still be a large gathering of family and friends on the day of the funeral. It won't be the joyous gathering they had all been looking forward to. The tables will still be full of food donated by friends. It may not be Paul's favorite foods like they had planned...but that doesn't matter now.

Bobby has made the necessary calls to delay his induction into the military due to his family emergency. Though he is having second thoughts, he wants desperately to avenge his brother's death.

Following the playing of Taps in a couple of weeks, the grieving will begin in earnest and the prayers for son number two will be prayed on humble knees.

Biographies of Contributing Authors

Bill Peterson was raised in Michigan's Upper Peninsula where he learned how to hunt and was taught by his father to make every shot count. Little did he know at the time that this training would be extremely useful within just a few short years.

His father, Gene was a B-17 pilot and spoke often of his hitch in the U.S. Air Corp. He instilled on his family a great sense of patriotism. At the age of eighteen, Bill not only enlisted and signed up to be a Huey helicopter crew chief, but when asked in Basic Training for his first and second choice of assignment, he said "Viet Nam". The sergeant asking the question was very surprised, but said that would be guaranteed. After watching helicopters in action on the nightly news, he wanted a part of it.

After thirty-six Air medals, (two with Valor), three Purple Hearts, and numerous other awards, he got more than he had hoped for.

Missions of Fire and Mercy is the story of his unit in Vietnam; C/227 Assault Helicopter Battalion, 1st Air Cavalry. His unit was responsible for supporting our U.S. Army, Special Forces, ARVN, Korean ROK troops, and other Allied troops. Charlie Company flew a potpourri of missions including, but not limited to: combat assault and recovery, support for troops in every way including ammo, food, water, and medevac missions, and aerial surveillance of battlegrounds before, during, and after the fight. BDA (Bomb Damage Assessment)...consisting of surveying what was left after B52 strikes and counting enemy bodies. The majority of these true, and all too often horrific incidents, took place between An Khe, the Central Highlands, Camp Evans in I Corp, the A Shau Valley, and Laos.

The goal of this story is to reach out to families and loved ones who never understood why their "soldier" has been so quiet about Viet Nam. Hopefully, this will help you to have a better first-hand view of those men and women, and what they went through. It is my hope that this will bring healing to those who served in combat, and help them realize that their memories are not faulty. These things did happen, and they can and should be proud to have served so honorably and bravely.

—William E. Peterson

Upon my retirement from the military I was not sure what I wanted to do. My first job was that of a tool lathe machine operator. After six months the walls were slowly coming in on me. I then decided to drive a tractor-trailer since I learned to drive one even before a car. My dad was a driver. After being away from home for twenty years in the military, I decided that I was gone too much while driving over the road. I then opened a carry out store. That was ok, but I wasn't making much money. I then got into security. After attending Community Police Academy I knew I wanted to do public community work. I was a police officer for fourteen years till my military service caught up to me and I had to retire100% due to health. Besides traveling, camping, and time with my wife, kids, and grandkids, I'm happy now with what I do. I love staying in touch with my Viet Nam brothers and enjoy the times when we can get together. Most of all my belief in God and our country is my mainstay.

—Larry Troxel

Chapter 2 *SADDLE UP*

After four trips to Viet Nam with the United States Navy, Ralph Christopher returned home to Richmond, Virginia, and attended classes at Virginia Commonwealth University. In 1982 he graduated the Musicians Institute in Hollywood, California, and is now a veteran performer and recording artist of over forty years. He is the author of four books, *River Rats, Duty Honor Sacrifice, Riverine,* and *Iron Butterfly,* and has spoken to the U.S. Navy on four occasions by invitation. He served as a lobbyist for Veterans Affairs and organized and built the Nevada State Veterans Memorial at the Nevada capital in Carson City as well as helped pass several bills supporting Veterans and their families. He now lives the good life in Las Vegas with his wife Deborah and his two beautiful daughters Alysia and Kayli and grandson Braydon and hosts a River Rats reunion every year for his brothers and friends.

—Ralph Christopher

Chapter 19 *DUNG ISLAND*

Joe holds a Doctor of Ministry in Missiology degree from Trinity International University – Deerfield, Illinois. He is a national and international conference speaker and author of *Battle Plan for Spiritual Warfare: God's Strategy for Overcoming the Enemy (Harvest House Publishers – 2004, now in its third printing).*

Serving as an Army helicopter pilot in Viet Nam from 1969-70, Joe was decorated with two Distinguished Flying Crosses and the Bronze Star. He also spent twelve years as a building contractor and real estate broker after Viet Nam before he and his wife, Kathy, became career missionaries with the Evangelical Free Church Mission in 1982. They have served as church planters in Africa, Guatemala, and Miami, Florida. They began serving Freedom in Christ Ministries (FICM) as International Directors in 1995 before becoming president of FICM from 2001 to 2006. In May of 2006, Joe transitioned out of the president's role to focus on a national and international marriage and family conference ministry and leadership development through their new ministry, *Living Legacy International.* The Wasmonds speak three languages.

Joe and Kathy have conducted conferences on resolving personal and spiritual conflicts, Christ-centered marriage retreats, discipleship/counseling, facilitated leadership retreats, and training for churches and mission agencies as well as a national reconciliation event for the government of Liberia in West Africa. Their ministry of evangelism and discipleship has taken them to more than sixty countries impacting people from all walks of life and worldviews, but especially Christian leaders, their families, military personnel and chaplains, churches, and organizations.

—Dr. Joe C. Wasmond
Chapter 19 *FRIENDLY FIRE*

Returning from Viet Nam, I bounced between medical and teaching occupations. Finding myself through service to Veterans, I became involved in the fight to recognize PTSD and Agent Orange. I was trained at American University in D.C. and worked as a service officer specializing in PTSD and appeals for a veteran's organization.

I have been diagnosed with untreatable PTSD.

—Mike Murphy "Doc"
Chapter 10 *DOC*

Postscript

When a patrol walked into the jaws of a vicious enemy ambush, it was sudden, short, and violent. There was incredible confusion with the rattle of machine guns, mortar, and grenade explosions. Tactical air strikes dropping napalm, bombs, strafing the enemy, and artillery strikes were necessary. Men who were just boys a few weeks or months before are now screaming for help while more bullets are buzzing past their heads. This raised the crescendo of battle and increased the adrenaline flow to a point that is never forgotten. The nightmares will be repeated for most of these warriors every day and night until they go to their graves.

As a Huey crew chief/gunner, my contact with the infantrymen was when I flew tactical missions in their support. When we escorted them mangled and bloody off the battlefield, I wondered when I would see them again...if I would see them again.

The camaraderie with one man willing to risk his life for another is a closeness that is indescribable. It is a feeling that is sorely missed once one returns to his home.

Chopper Warriors shows you what these "kids" went through. What you have read are real life and death accounts of our tours in Viet Nam.

Anyone who has known war; be it a combatant, a civilian adult, or a child is forever changed by the experience. What they have known is a weight they will each carry for the rest of their lives.

Glossary

AAA: Anti-aircraft fire.

Angel Flight: Fixed wing aircraft. Often C130s used for transportation of soldiers' remains back to the United States. These are extremely solemn flights.

AO: Area of Operations.

Blacked Out: Navigation Lights Out.

Brown Arc: Pucker factor in the brown arc meant you were very Scared.

"Bulletholes 67": One of author's nicknames.

CA: Combat assault.

Click: 1,000 meters.

Concertina Wire: Razor sharp barbed wire laid around perimeter in long coils.

Cs Gas: Tear gas.

Danger Close: Way too close for comfort. There were occasions when in imminent danger of being overrun that ground units would call in an airstrike on their own position.

Dust Off: Medevac.

FAC: Forward Air Controller .

Frag: Fragmentation grenade.

Gaggle: A flight or formation of several aircraft.

Ground Guide: Person on the ground guiding an aircraft in for landing.

Gunship: Aircraft armed with guns - The Huey helicopter has two pairs of rocket pods holding thirty-six rockets each – one mini-gun and a 20mm canon.

Grunt: Ground soldier in the boonies.

KIA: Killed in action.

Lister Bag: Canvas bag approximately thirty gallons with spigots for holding water, suspended from three poles.

Loach: Nickname given to the OH6 by flight crews which is a single-engine light helicopter that has a four-bladed main rotor. It was used for scouting, observation, escort and attack missions.

LOH: Light Observation Helicopter.

LRRP: Long range recon patrol.

LT: Lieutenant.

LZ: Landing Zone.

M16: Semi-auto 5.56 mm rifle.

M60: Semi-auto 7.62 machine gun.

MIA: Missing in action.

Navy Corpsman: Navy medic usually based in the field.

NVA: North Vietnamese Army.

O-1 Bird Dog: Single engine, tandem, high wing observation airplane. It usually carried several marking rockets under the wing for marking targets, sometimes carried an M60 machine gun.

On the deck: Low level flying over the trees and rice paddies. Nap of the earth.

"Pete": Author's nickname.

Pickles: Slang for when a pilot drops a bomb. He "pickles" his load – perhaps so-called because the bombs are shaped like pickles?

Pop Smoke: A smoke grenade of various colors was thrown to mark a position on the ground.

PRC25: Field Radio used by the grunts.

Pucker factor in the brown arc: When a soldier was scared so bad, his rear end was puckered up. The brown arc meant he was really scared.

Puff: C47 fixed wing transport aircraft with three mini guns mounted on the left side, each capable of firing 6,000 rounds per minute with every fifth one a tracer. It could orbit a unit under attack and accurately lay down a wall of fire wiping out the enemy. When operating at night, its stream of bullets looked like a dragon's fiery breath.

PZ: Pick up zone.

Ranger: Specially trained airborne soldier.

RTO: Radio Telephone Operator in the field who carried the PRC25 field radio.

Satchel charge: Enemy homemade grenade.

Search And Destroy: Search out the enemy and destroy him and the area he was in.

Shooting ports: Holes in bunker wall like windows for shooting out of.

SITREP: Situation report. Generally referred to an enemy situation at the time.

Six: Designation for ground or air commander. Usually with a rank of Captain or above.

Slick: Huey for carrying troops. Armed with two M60 machine guns.

TAC: Tactical air. Aerial fighters/bombers.

Top: Sergeant in charge in the company area.

Torques: Nickname given to the crew chiefs/gunners on the OH6.

Track: To manually balance the rotor blades if there was excessive vibration.

VR: Visual reconnaissance.

Wart Hog: Air Force A10 fighter/bomber. Slower than most fighter jets, but was able to deliver payload more accurately.

WIA: Wounded in action.

Willy Pete: White phosphorous grenade or artillery round. This had a distinct white smoke so was easily identified. Easily started fires and caused secondary explosions when dropped on enemy munitions.

Your Six: "I have your six" refers to someone watching your back.

27599013R00088

Made in the USA
Charleston, SC
16 March 2014